# I, THE LAWYER

## BY LUIS KUTNER

**Prose:**

THE ADMIRAL
*In collaboration with Laurin Hall Healy*

LIFE IN TWELVE MINUTES
*In collaboration with W. T. Brannan*

WORLD HABEAS CORPUS

THE GREATER LOVE

I, THE LAWYER

**Poetry:**

FLIGHTS AND CASCADES

RED WINE AND SHADOWS

MOONSPLASHED

**Law Journal Articles:**

*International Due Process of Law; United Nations Writ of Habeas Corpus; World Habeas Corpus—A Legal Absolute for Survival; Habeas Proprietatem: Due Process for International Investment; World Habeas Corpus for International Man: A Credo for International Due Process of Law; Unfair Comment: A Warning to News Media; The Illusion of Due Process in Commitment Proceedings; Due Process of Economy; World Habeas Corpus and International Extradition; Due Process of Outer Space Law: Proposed International Cosmos Court; Anti-Trust Control of Labor*

# I, THE LAWYER

by Luis Kutner

ILLUSTRATED

DODD, MEAD & COMPANY

NEW YORK

Library of Congress Catalog Card Number: 66-12026
Printed in the United States of America
by The Cornwall Press, Inc., Cornwall, N. Y.

THIS BOOK IS DEDICATED TO

Dean Emeritus Roscoe Pound
Professor Quincy Wright
Professor Myres S. McDougal
Professor Harold D. Lasswell
Honorable Charles S. Rhyne
Associate United States Justice
William J. Brennan, Jr.
Judge Caroline K. Simon
Chief Judge William J. Campbell
Judge James B. Parsons
Honorable Paul G. Hoffman
Justice Kotaro Tanaka, International
Court of Justice

to name but a few who have faith that Human Rights in a "universal society without universal law" can be established on one of the common standards and procedures like WORLD HABEAS CORPUS.

# Acknowledgments

My debt is acknowledged to those who have labored in my legal vineyard. The philosophy, attitudes and tenacity for public service were influenced by many who privileged me with their devotion to an ordered society. This book, in many ways, reflects the distillation of their attitudes and influence upon my development as a lawyer.

To mention but a few, I include Dean Roscoe Pound of Harvard, the great architect of law and versatile innovator in legal reforms; Professor Quincy Wright, the eminent international teacher and scholar, whose optimism for a world rule of law is tempered with a scholarly boldness and caution; Professor Harold D. Lasswell, whose pyrotechnic brilliance and achievements in political science and in the law, and other fields, set many goals which have been my sustained inspiration; Professor Myres S. McDougal, whose Mount Everest achievements in the many fields of world public order are awesome, but always ready to counsel and encourage; and to Bill Brannon my unrestrained gratitude for his devotion to the project of this book.

# Why This Book?

This book was written to provide some helpful answers for the searching inquiry into the choosing of a career. At the same time, it rounds out an innate decision to try to be of service to one's fellow man. Tomorrow should be a better place because of even one more lawyer's activating presence and modest contribution to the future generations.

My fellow lawyers and I are enthusiastically sold on our profession. This contagious pleasure should be spread to the potential participants in public affairs. It is a world of fascination and satisfaction. One can wear the well-concealed armor of a Sir Galahad in helping to conquer the dragons of evil and injustice.

Within the limits of brevity, this book explores the systematic evolution of the ground rules in an ordered society. This is the heart and core of law. Simply stated, law is a rule of conduct. It prohibits and punishes "hurtful" conduct. Contrariwise, it furnishes the road signs for permissive and "nonhurtful" conduct.

Primitive man evolved traditions and stern codes for human survival. Experience was the teacher. The daily welfare of a family and social group in a hostile physical world was basic.

Early law, beginning in trial and error, developed ethics ranging from vindictive cruelty to the present-day goals of Judaism, Christianity and Western civilization.

Law resolves that a decent and dignified and peaceful world can endure only on the principle that all created men are equal before it. This equation is paramount, regardless of color or creed or religious belief. This truth is absolute. Law must be based and administered on the concept of equal justice and humanity for all. "We are our brother's keeper" must be concretely implemented.

It is an inexorable law of nature that all men are *not* created equal as far as intelligence, talent, size, stature, economic and social strata are concerned. Saying that all men are equal is not meant to adjudicate that they are equal in the foregoing respects. It would, of course, be naive to take any such premise for granted. What is meant, rather, is that in a civilized community all men must be treated as equal before the law. Man has progressed from the elementary to the chronologically sophisticated; from simple nomadic rules to the threshold of outer-space law.

If this book inspires the readers to study law formally and join this profession of service, it also suggests that there might be further study-in-depth. The fascination is boundless. The law will become your pervading motivation in life. You will be angered at unjust laws. You will seek to expand the just laws. You will strive toward a goal where dictatorial law, based on the strong will of a tyrant, readily gives way to the reasonable rules of the common experiences of man seeking right and justice.

The scope of law is tremendous. It finds its way everywhere in the broad fields of human knowledge and experience. It is involved in ethics, medicine, history, philosophy, sociology, anthropology, eugenics, psychology and religion. I hope that in sharing my own knowledge and experience in law with others interested in the field I have partially paid my debt to a multi-faceted, challenging and rewarding vocation.

LUIS KUTNER

# Contents

# Illustrations

## Following page 80

Abraham Lincoln, as a young lawyer, and the interior and exterior of the old courthouse at Pekin, Illinois, where he practiced frequently before becoming President of the United States.

This figure, which symbolizes "Turning the Wheel of the Law" to the Buddhists, is located at Benares, India.

The upper part of the Code of Hammurabi (about 2100 B.C.), now in the Louvre, Paris, France. The King, Amraphel in the Old Testament, stands before the sun-god Shamash to receive the laws.

Symbolic picture of Moses holding the Tablets of the Laws of God, the Ten Commandments.

Charles the Bold, Duke of Burgundy, dispenses legal decisions personally in 1473.

A German law court in session in 1575. The judges wear berets, the lawyers are bareheaded.

*The Trial* is pictured by "Phiz" for *Pickwick Papers*, by Charles Dickens.

This humorous sketch of the 1800's is titled *Attorney and Client, Fortitude and Impatience.*

Informality vs. formality in holding court. The old steel engraving above pictures a justice of the peace comfortably holding court in his home, with a dapper young lawyer pleading his case. The drawing below shows the United States District Court Room in the new Post Office Building, in New York City, during the 1870's.

Through law, a country is firmly established in freedom and a world is united for universal justice.

This sculptured panel by Lee Lawrie, in the Nebraska State Capitol, pictures the drafting of the Constitution of the United States.

The International Court of Justice in session at The Hague.

The Supreme Court Room in Washington, D. C., and two panels of the sculptured frieze by Adolph A. Weinman. At the top is "Majesty of the Law and Power of Government," with, below it, "Triumph of Justice with Divine Guidance."

PART **I**

———

THIS
IS
THE LAW

# 1. The Law, a Noble Profession

When you retire at bedtime, you sleep better knowing that representatives of the law are patrolling the streets and highways. When you start out from home in the morning or return in the afternoon or evening, your chief concern is with the normal rules of traffic safety regulating both vehicles and pedestrians. It seldom occurs to you how great the danger to your life might be without speed limits and traffic lights.

If you decide to to shopping, you know that you can expect to buy products of uniform quality and that they most likely will be what the label says they are. Everybody will be treated equally while in the shops.

For a holiday, you may decide on a trip to a distant city. On the way, you will receive certain services and accept them as your due. In a strange city, you will meet people who will be very friendly, who will try to help you enjoy your visit, although you have never seen them before.

When your holiday time is up, you will return home again with little or no thought of any hazard and take up your normal life where you left off.

Today, all this is routine and you think nothing of it. But it was not always so.

In days gone by, this comfortable way of life did not exist. Consider these conditions:

Thieving prowlers were common and at least one dog was kept in every home to sound the alarm. Even so, the head of the house usually went to bed with a loaded shotgun within easy reach. There were few policemen and some communities had none at all. Holdup bandits infested the highways and even the railroads and every traveler ventured forth at his own risk.

Shopping in an unknown store was an adventure in which the unwary buyer could be cheated at the whim of the owner. The top price for any item was the highest amount the merchant or his clerk could persuade the buyer to pay.

The maker of a product put forth any sort of false claim for his ware without fear of punishment. For example, a garment might be marked to show that it was handmade of the finest imported material, although it actually was very cheap and had been put together in a sweatshop in the same city. The producer of a drug could label it any way he chose, even though it might be worthless or perhaps harmful. In those uncertain days, it was up to the purchaser to make sure that he got what he paid for.

Any kind of long journey used to be beset with peril. The traveler was lucky if he reached his destination safely and without losing some of his possessions on the way. He was even luckier if he managed to visit a strange city and complete the return trip without danger.

Of course, much of that uncertainty has changed for the better. Some of this is due to scientific progress—but not all.

The law is responsible for most of the change. It has provided police protection for nearly everybody—even in the smallest communities. That's why you can go to bed at night without having to lie awake and worry about nighttime danger, why you can drive along a country road without fear that you will be stopped by a highwayman; why you can journey anywhere in the United States and Canada with the knowledge that you are being protected by the law.

In addition to its purpose of defending you from bodily harm at the hands of criminals, the law has advanced in many other protective ways—and much of this improvement has occurred within the lifetimes of people who are still living.

In America, the years around the turn of the century were a period of wild expansion, with many new railroads being built, new factories springing up in hundreds of communities, and the last of the frontiers being opened to what we call civilization.

Although this was a time of great progress in the history of the United States—and Canada too—it also was a period when a few greedy men, gluttonous for power, managed to gain control of large tracts of land and huge industries. In so doing, they ruled the lives of hundreds of thousands of poor people. Men and women, even children, were forced to spend most of their waking hours in hard labor—or starve.

There were other abuses. Bribery of public officials was pretty common. An unscrupulous man with great power and wealth could do almost anything he wanted to because there were no laws to stop him.

Fortunately, about that time, there were thousands of young men who could see the need for new laws and the many opportunities that lay ahead for the man with legal training—not only for helping themselves, but for improving the conditions of others as well, by the passing of laws to limit the powers of the mighty.

A century had been devoted to making laws to protect the basic rights of the individual in matters of personal safety and to secure private property, but little had been done to combat the new frauds and dangers that were resulting from the industrial expansion.

The new crop of young lawyers, aided by the tried and true wisdom of many able older attorneys, set out to correct some of the wrongs, especially those developing in business and commerce.

Consider some of the changes for the protection of mankind that have been brought about in no more than half a century:

The maker of pills and tonics no longer can claim falsely that his remedies will cure anything from a cold to cancer. Before it can be sold to the public, each medicine must pass rigid tests by the expert chemists and doctors serving the Food and Drug Administration of the United States Government.

Laws prevent the sale, without a doctor's order, of harmful drugs that may cause the consumer to become an addict and eventually die a horrible death.

Other laws prevent dishonest manufacturers from labeling

products, such as canned and packaged foods, to make them appear to be something they are not.

Among the most important laws of the twentieth century are those relating to trusts. A trust is a combination of companies, all under the same management, sometimes designed to eliminate all competition. If one company controlled the entire supply of one product or service, it could charge any price it chose, regardless of the actual value. The antitrust laws put a stop to that by promoting competitive trade.

There are many other laws to protect the honest person and the honest business against those who would be dishonest.

All these protective regulations, whose purpose is to do the most good for the most people, have established through the efforts of men and women who practice law.

This is my reason for believing that the law is a noble profession.

PART **II**

—

# HISTORY
# OF
# THE LAW

# 2. The Jews and the Beginning of Law

As far as we know, the law began with the family. The father was the head of the family and the orders he gave, the rules of conduct made by him, were the law.

As families expanded and the members went out on their own, the family group became known as a clan, subject to the rule of the man who was selected to head it. Eventually clans in the same area joined forces and became members of a tribe. A chief was chosen to head this larger group.

The chief of the tribe made rules or laws to govern the dealings of one clan with another, but the head of the clan still made the laws for the family group. If a tribal laws was broken, the chief decided the guilt or innocence of the person accused and fixed the punishment. The head of a clan judged and decided punishment for those who broke his rules within his family group.

Those clan and tribal laws were not written

down for countless centuries—we don't know just how many
—but they were handed down by word of mouth from one
generation to another. Some of them are actually still in
force today. For example, a man who was a member of one
clan could not marry a woman from the same clan; his bride
must be chosen from another clan that was part of the
tribe.

In those ancient times, there were few property rights.
It was considered that all the land was owned by God and
that it could be used by the members of any tribe who settled
on it. Farming, hunting and fishing were the main ways of
making a living then, and the tribes moved around a great
deal. After a tract of land had been worked for a few generations, the tribe went on to look for richer soil and settled
somewhere else. Wars of subjugation were avoided whenever possible.

When a tribe moved, the laws of the old land became the
laws of the new land. These laws were changed or new laws
were made only as the wanderers found new traits in freshly
occupied lands—or as the habits of the people changed. Still,
the laws were by word of mouth and not written because
writing, even on stone tablets, had not yet been invented.

The first written law that we know about was that of
Moses, who led the Jews out of bondage in Egypt on a
journey that lasted forty years. During that time, Moses
wrote the laws that governed the Jews, both in their religious
and their social lives. The law of Moses was the framework
on which most Jewish law was built. Some believed that it
was written by Moses, others that Moses merely made a
record of rules given to him by God.

The most important of the laws of Moses are the Ten

Commandments. Four of these are religious, but the other six were the basis of nearly all later social laws. From these and other laws of Moses grew the laws of ancient Greece and Rome and later of England—and from all these came the basic laws of the United States.

Perhaps the most important laws stemmed from the Commandments, "Thou shalt not kill," "Thou shalt not steal," "Thou shalt not bear false witness" and "Thou shalt not covet."

The Commandment against coveting is the first written law that deals with property rights and from it have developed a large number of laws governing business and commerce. During the 3,300 years since Moses first gave this Commandment to the Jews, thousands of laws that can be traced to it have been written and put in force. These include many of America's laws of commerce that are valid today.

Ruling and making laws for the large number of Jews whom Moses was leading to the Promised Land during a trip that lasted forty years was too much for one man. Moses needed help and, according to the Bible:

". . . Moses chose able men out of all Israel, and made them heads over the people, rulers of thousands, rulers of hundreds, rulers of fifties, and rulers of tens.

"And they judged the people at all seasons; the hard cases they brought unto Moses, but every small matter they judged themselves."

Thus, Moses began a judicial system that is not too different from many of those in effect more than 3,000 years later. Way back in those days, a law violation was tried according to how serious it was, the tough cases going to Moses, who constituted the Supreme Court of that day.

Altogether, Moses wrote five books of laws that came to be known as the Torah. This was a set of rules, both legal and religious, to guide the conduct of the Jewish people, and it is still widely used by people of the Jewish faith.

For more than 500 years after the death of Moses, his laws continued in effect and were added to by many Jewish officials. Gradually, a new system came into being. The land occupied by a tribe was divided among the clans who, in turn, divided it among the individual families. But every fiftieth year, known as the jubilee, was a period of rest, when slaves were freed, debts were forgiven, and the land went back to the tribe, to be divided again among the clans and families. The people spent their normal working time reading and learning the laws.

The rulers still were the judges and there were no lawyers, but there were wise men who helped the rulers to soften many of the harsh regulations set down by Moses. About the seventh century B.C., money was coined and was used to buy and sell land and other property. To some extent, the use of money replaced the system of swapping that had been the only means of doing business up to then.

With money in use, it was possible to hire people to do work and to go into debt for goods on a promise to pay. But the law remained firm on one point—there could be no usury. As we know it today, the term usury means "lending money at a rate of interest that is too high." But to the Jews of that period, any loaning of money for payment of a fee was usury and was considered illegal.

Great progress was made. Many people left the farms;

towns and cities were built. Trades and crafts, such as those of carpenter, innkeeper, mason, and the like, became common. Jerusalem developed into a thriving city.

In 597 B.C., the progress of the Jews was halted suddenly by the invasion of a powerful army from Babylon. Jerusalem was destroyed and about 4,000 Jews were exiled to Babylon, where they lived for about fifty years. Then a Persian king, Cyrus, conquered Babylon and freed the Jews so that they could return to their homeland and rebuild Jerusalem.

During the centuries that followed, there were several invasions and the Jews were forced to live under the rule of a conquering army. They were, in turn, under the yokes of the Persians, the Egyptians, the Syrians and the Romans.

But the Jews had a great thirst for knowledge, and the oppressors could not stop their efforts to learn. A group of men referred to in the Old Testament as priests, elders and scribes began a study that they called the Mishnah. (Today, it would be labeled a project and probably would be known as Operation Mishnah.) The purpose was to study the laws written by Moses and those after him; to inquire into the history, culture and lore of the Jews and to try to separate fact from myth.

The knowledge gained in the Mishnah would be compiled and, in time, would be put in writing to guide the Jews in all phases of their lives—religious, social, business and legal.

The men engaged in the Mishnah formed an assembly known as the Great Sanhedrin. It was led by a president and a vice president and had seventy-one members, considered the wisest leaders in the land. They not only read and interpreted the laws, but set up courts for the trials of all cases.

The elders of the Great Sanhedrin were the judges, and the scribes were the lawyers.

Their aims was to be fair and just and they soon realized there was a great difference between civil lawsuits and criminal trials. Three judges could try a civil suit—usually a dispute over property between two persons—and a verdict by two of the three judges was binding.

But to try a criminal case, there must be twenty-three judges and the verdict was in favor of the accused if only twelve of the judges voted to convict him. If thirteen or more voted against him, he was convicted. During the trial, the prosecutor could call on only those witnesses who could testify directly against the accused. But the defense could call any number of witnesses to vouch for his character, whether or not they knew anything of the crime.

The judges were so anxious that the accused have a fair trial, the hearing might be delayed for days, even weeks, to give him an opportunity to produce more evidence.

Usually, the outside power that was ruling the Jews allowed them to hold trials and punish their own people. But the Romans would not permit the Jews to inflict the death penalty. Nor would the Romans allow them to put their religious beliefs in writing. Since the edicts of the Mishnah mixed religion and law, much of their work was passed on to others by men known as the repeaters.

Some writing was done in secret by the scribes and, in time, the law against writing by the Jews was disregarded so that the knowledge of centuries and the laws could be preserved.

Schools of different grades, from the elementary to the university level, were started. Men who had gained knowledge from the members of the Great Sanhedrin were the teachers. There were no textbooks, but the pupils were taught to read and write and to think for themselves. In the universities, the teachers spent only part of the time in lecturing. If students had questions, these were discussed and debated by the teacher and any student who wanted to take part.

Many new ideas emerged and the best were added to the store of knowledge being collected by the Mishnah. But it was about 1,000 years before the scribes finally put the accumulated knowledge of the Mishnah into writing in a work known as the Talmud, a classic that is widely read and studied today because of the wisdom it contains.

It was during this period in Jewish history that Jesus Christ was born. It was he who was to have a great influence on the moral—and therefore the legal—standards of future generations.

By any test, Jesus was remarkable. According to the New Testament, he disappeared once when he was twelve years old and when his parents found him three days later, he was in the temple, discussing and debating the Jewish laws with a group of learned priests and elders. Even at twelve, he had a firm understanding of the laws.

Jesus Christ voiced the Golden Rule, "Do unto others as you would have them do unto you." Twenty centuries later, this still is the greatest guide to human conduct ever devised. If every person abided by this simple rule, there would be no need for much of the great mass of law that exists today.

Although Jesus was well aware of the laws of Moses and his successors and his teachings were based on them, he knew that they often were too stern. He preached kindness,

tolerance, humility, brotherhood, charity, honor and un-
selfishness.

A new religion, Christianity, was based on his teachings,
which developed from the earlier beliefs of the Jews. And
his teachings have been the foundation of many of today's
laws.

# 3. The Laws of the Ancient Greeks

What we know of the ancient Greeks is to be found mostly in the works of Homer, a storyteller who wrote of the laws while relating the history of his people. Consequently, the laws of the ancient Greeks have come to be known as Homeric Law. To understand their laws, we must know something of their history and their customs.

The people who settled in Greece came from states near the homeland of the Jews. They spoke an Aryan language which was very much like that of the Jews, and their system of clans and tribes was also quite similar, at least in the beginning.

The Greeks occupied many places around the Mediterranean Sea. In addition to what now is known as Greece, they settled in much of Sicily and along the southern coast of Italy. They formed many independent cities, the largest and most important of which were Athens and Sparta, which

actually were city-states, since they took in the rural areas
around them.

Early in the growth of the Greek states, probably about
800 B.C., the clans developed a form of democracy that is
similar in some ways to the democracies of today. The head
of the clan was the ruler. However, other men wanted a
voice in government, so the heads of families formed a council (comparable to a state senate), while other men in the
clan formed an assembly (comparable to a state house of
representatives). The head of the clan was the president, the
council and the assembly were the legislature. Although the
men of the council were important as heads of their families,
they could make no law without the consent of the assembly.

This was democracy for the upper crust or ruling class,
but there were many people who had no voice at all in making the laws or running the government. These were the
people who had moved to Greece from other countries, employees of the clans, and slaves. Even after a kindly master
freed a slave and he became known as a freedman, he still
did not have the right to vote or hold office.

Athens grew and became the capital of a state called
Attica. (Today, Attica is a Greek state and Athens is the
capital.) Eleven other small, independent states joined Attica, which was the most populous of the Greek nations. The
Greeks were thirsty for knowledge and Athens soon was the
center of culture and learning of the world as it was known
then.

Up to that time, all laws had been oral and subject to the
members of the councils or assemblies. They were believed
to be of divine origin, made not only to settle disputes and
punish crimes, but also to please the gods. There were thou-

sands of Greek gods, each clan having its own. It was believed that the deities frowned upon moving about, so a Greek family seldom moved. There was also a theory that the gods liked privacy. Each house was built with ample space between it and the next one.

But with the growth of the cities, especially Athens, and the increase in population, there was some doubt about the oral laws. They were collected and put in writing in 664 B.C. by a group of lawmen who removed some of the references to the gods and reshaped them to relate more to the affairs of the people. But they kept much of the pomp and most of the rites and ceremonies attendant upon legal procedures. Some of these formalities are still with us today, although they are simpler.

To manage the business of Attica, nine governors were chosen. One of them had the title of king. But the king did not have the great power that kings of later periods wielded in other countries. He presided at meetings of the governors and directed trials at which the governors passed on the more serious crimes, or major violations of the laws of trade. Lesser legal matters were tried by the councils and clan assemblies.

Punishments varied. A person who was convicted might be fined or he might be flogged or put to death. For several centuries, a whole family had to answer for the crime of one of its members. If the family was found guilty, one of the sons could be sent into exile in another country.

The Greeks carried on brisk trade and many of those involved went into debt. Sometimes, they had mortgages on their farms and homes. It was not unusual for a man to offer his person as security for a loan. If he couldn't pay, he might

be sold into slavery—and there were cases where his entire
family was forced to go with him.

These practices almost resulted in ruin to the state. If a
farmer lost his land because he couldn't pay the debt on it,
he and his family moved to the city. Others who couldn't
exist on the income from their farms also moved to Athens.

Soon, the metropolis was overflowing with thousands of
the poor who had no means of making a living. The ruling
classes realized that these desperate people were about to
revolt and something must be done to remedy the situation.
A man named Draco was hired to write new laws.

Draco started out right. He set up a specific legal procedure, with courts to deal with all cases. He also gave the
right to vote to many who had never been permitted to vote
before.

But his punishments were so harsh that they soon out-
weighed the good he had done. The penalty for almost any
crime, even petty theft, was death. His punishments were so
cruel that the name Draconian is applied to any unusually
harsh law today. If a man had no job, he lost his vote; if a
man without a job was from a foreign country, he was put to
death.

It seemed that revolt was brewing again among the im-
poverished, and the wealthy had to do something to prevent
it and satisfy the people. The man they chose to succeed
Draco was Solon, who seemed satisfactory to all concerned.

Solon had inherited wealth and he had spent it when he
was still a young man. He was forced to go to work, but that
didn't make him lose his zest for life. He was successful in
business and, before long, built up another fortune. He had a
national reputation for honesty. He traveled to other coun-

tries, where he studied their laws and customs. As a result of all this, he was known for his wisdom and many asked his advice.

Because he was rich and wise, the wealthy approved of him. The poor liked him because he was honest. He began his new job of restoring order to Attica about 594 B.C. By agreement of the people, he was made a dictator.

His first act was to cut down all personal debts and to erase some of them. The practice of borrowing money and using the person as security was outlawed. The slaves were freed and those who had been banished to other lands were brought back wherever possible.

But there still was much to do. Solon limited the amount of land any man could own and, consequently, some wealthy men had to give up large tracts. This provided enough land for those who had none, but the new farmers still had to exist. Solon prohibited the sale of food outside Attica until new harvests brought an ample supply.

He set up rules for doing business, which included contracts for labor and contracts for the sale of property, as well as for corporations. Although this still was a comparatively primitive age, the hard-working Greeks were shrewd businessmen. The corporate structures they devised had many of the elements of a corporation of today. The Greek corporations are the first of which we have any record and they have been models for similar business systems down through the centuries.

Solon voided all of Draco's penal laws except those dealing with murder and tyranny. He decreed punishments according to the seriousness of the crimes. These ranged from fines to flogging or lashing to exile. There were few prison sentences.

Solon set up a new government, composed of a Council and an Assembly. The Council had 400 members, elected by the people; the Assembly was composed of all citizens who wanted to participate. Every new law was started by the citizens in the Assembly. If it was approved by a majority of the Assembly, it went to the Council for final action.

Trial by jury as established by Solon was a lot different from today's jury trial. Six thousand persons were chosen to act as jurors for a term of one year, and they were the body from which jurors for all trials were selected. The number of jurors in any case was never less than 500 and sometimes there were as many as 2,000 to act at a trial. The judge was chosen by lot from among the jurors and he was nothing more than a presiding officer.

There were no prosecutors and no judges trained in the law. Nor was there a grand jury. Any citizen could indict any other person by putting the charge in writing. The accuser acted as his own prosecutor and the man on trial defended himself. As soon as they had finished, the judge called for a vote. If it was a civil case (that is, one involving business, debt, or the like), and the jury found in favor of the accuser, it was up to him to recover his loss. The government did not do it for him. But the government did inflict the penalty in a criminal case.

Since most of the people concerned at a trial, including the judge and the jurors, knew little about the laws, men who did know them were hired to explain them to the members of the juries, who could interpret them any way they chose. The judge did not have the power to set aside a verdict of a jury; in fact, he did not know enough about the laws to do so if he had had the power.

In time, orators were hired by the principals in a trial to write speeches about the case and address the jury. Orators soon learned many methods of swaying juries and, in effect, became the lawyers of that day.

Solon wrote a complete set of laws and they pleased the people. Before he resigned, he exacted a pledge from the Atticans that they would not change his laws for a hundred years. Actually, Solon's laws remained in effect for five hundred years, with certain changes.

After he had resigned and gone away from the country on a trip that lasted ten years, the first of several tyrants seized power and ruled the Atticans. But the reigns of these tyrants did not last long and, eventually, the democratic form of government was restored in Attica.

One Greek who did not approve of democracy established his own rule in Sparta. His name was Lycurgus. He set out to produce a master race and, in order to accomplish this, took boys from their homes when they were eight years old. They were put together in barracks where they were forced to go through a hardening process. They slept on very rough beds or on the ground. They were taught reading and writing, but their most important lessons were in how to endure pain. This was expected to give them courage.

Although Sparta had a government, Lycurgus actually took control through his unusual powers of persuasion. There was a senate, composed of wealthy men over sixty years of age, and an assembly whose members were free men over thirty.

Members of the senate were elected in a very strange way. A candidate would appear before a gathering of citizens and

would be applauded. Other candidates also would stand before the group and wait for the hand clapping. The twenty-
eight men who received the most applause were elected to
the senate to become the country's chief law-making body!

But, after Lycurgus became dictator, the laws that the
senate passed were only those that the new ruler wanted. He
set up a secret police to make sure that every person did his
bidding.

As stated, the aim of Lycurgus was to create a master race
which would be so tough and strong that they would rule
the world. The hardening ordeal that the boys went through
did, in fact, make them a bit tougher than their neighbors.
The Spartans invaded Athens and conquered its people,
holding sway for a few decades. During this period, Sparta
was the greatest military power on earth.

But the city of Thebes, which had developed its own
army, invaded Athens in 371 B.C., forcing out the Spartans.
Lycurgus had left Sparta, after asking the people not to
change his laws. Afraid to go back, he starved to death. The
master race–police state that he had set up failed, just as
another, set up by Adolf Hitler, was to fail some twenty-four
centuries later.

In Athens, during the years 463-399 B.C., there lived a
man who has been called one of the wisest human beings of
all time. His name was Socrates. He started out as a sculptor,
but he gave this up for what he called a search for the truth.
Much of his adult life was spent in his never-ending quest.

He would stop a young man on the street and, if the other
would spend the time with him, he might devote a few
minutes, a few hours, or a day, questioning some simple statement the man had made. Through many questions concern-

ings the words and subjects brought up during the conversation, he would probe the mind of the other man. Nearly always, he managed to prove that the original statements made by the other man were false. But, along the way, his persistent, though gentle, questioning brought out many facts, known to him or to the other—and ultimately known to both when the explored facts had been brought to light.

Socrates claimed that he was very ignorant and that he wanted to learn through what amounted to cross-examination. But his main purpose really was to develop the mind of any young man who would stand still for a session of his questioning. Many of his queries were long and they revealed that Socrates was both wise and learned. . . . After a long dialogue with him, the other man was wiser, too.

Although Socrates had no organized school, many young men became his pupils, following him about the streets in a group and learning by listening every time he managed to collar a passer-by and engage him in an argument. He developed the art of cross-examination much as it is taught in law schools today and is used by good trial lawyers.

Socrates considered any young man who wanted to learn as his pupil. The pupil would state a problem and Socrates would proceed to tear it apart through cross-examinatioin. He often said that he wanted to develop the minds of the young, and he did that by teaching them to think and to examine everything in the light of reason.

He was perhaps the first to insist that a law was not necessarily good because it was the law a year ago or a hundred years ago. Could it be changed or improved? Would it stand up if it were tested by logic and reason?

(The founding fathers who wrote the United States Constitution recognized this principle when they provided for amendments. They knew that the Constitution was not perfect, that, in time and under different circumstances, perhaps wiser men might have good reason to make changes.)

One of the most devoted pupils of Socrates was Plato, who established a school in Athens that continued for nine hundred years. It offered every known subject—reading, writing, the recognized sciences, philosophy, law and government.

But Plato didn't depend on lectures or standard lessons. Like Socrates, he believed that knowledge is gained through individual learning. He would set up a problem for his pupils, then tell them to solve it through the critical analysis and questioning that he had absorbed from Socrates—he added something to the methods of Socrates.

The students could tear a problem apart and find all that was wrong with it. However, that was only half of the lesson. Subsequently, through the same type of logic and reasoning, developed usually by cross-examination, they had to find the answer to the problem. This intensive method is similar to scientific and medical research of all kinds carried on in our laboratories today.

Both Socrates and Plato developed some degree of logic, but it was Plato's pupil, Aristotle, who perfected it. He devised a rule that is as good today as it was then, about 2,200 years ago, and it is used often in law. It is called a syllogism and consists of a major premise and a minor premise that lead to a conclusion. For example:

MAJOR PREMISE:    All persons are human beings.
MINOR PREMISE:    I am a person.
CONCLUSION:       Therefore, I am a human being.

To be valid, a major premise must be a general truth. And to reach the right conclusion, the minor premise must be properly related to the major premise. This is known as syllogistic reasoning and it is widely used by lawyers today. It has not been changed in any way since it first was developed by Aristotle. It is similar to certain laws of nature or science, such as gravity—time has not changed these, either.

Other Greeks contributed to the growth of the law, but none so much as Socrates, Plato and Aristotle, who gave us some sound ideas that are still in use. Solon is remembered mostly because of his power and the great number of laws he enacted. Today, we often refer to a lawmaker as a solon.

# 4. The Roman Lawmakers

Until about 500 B.C., the Romans were ruled by kings. When the last one was shorn of power, a republic was established, but it was far different from a republic or democracy as we know it today. It was ruled by the citizens of Rome, but the hitch was that the great majority of residents, known as plebeians, did not have the rights of citizens, could not vote and had no voice in the government.

In its make-up, the Roman Republic was somewhat similar to the government of the United States. There was a Senate, composed of heads of the leading families, and they were elected by the aristocrats. But the Senate could not act without the lower house, the Assembly, whose members came from the lower classes of Roman citizens.

The government was headed by not one but two men called consuls, probably because it was their duty to counsel and consult with the Senate and Assembly, just as the President of the United States today advises Congress and often tries to sway its members.

Other important officials were the praetors, or magistrates, who held trials and passed judgment.

In many ways, the Roman laws were similar to those of the Greeks. It seems likely that Roman leaders traveled to Greece, while Greek lawmakers visited Rome, and that they exchanged views. This resulted in the best—or sometimes the worst—laws being adopted by both countries. In each, the laws helped the rich and hurt the lower classes.

The plebeians didn't like this and, as their numbers grew, they began to realize their power—they were the people who were doing most of the work. They decided to flex their muscles and went on strike. Since there was nobody to do the work, they were recognized by the upper classes in a way that persuaded them to call off the strike. The office of tribune was created to appease the plebeians. At first, there were three of these officials but, as the commoners gained more rights, ten tribunes in all were elected to represent them without any participation by the Senate.

The tribunes were, for a time, the most powerful officials in Rome. They had the power of the veto over almost any official act. One of them had merely to forbid an act and it became void.

But the patricians found a way to get around this. Patricians themselves became tribunes to represent the lower class. Thus, their rulings favored the upper classes more often than they did the plebeians. Despite this, the power of the lower classes grew with their numbers and, about 200 B.C., they were permitted to vote and hold office.

Even so, the aristocrats continued to control the government by putting up candidates who talked the cause of the commoners but, after they were elected, more often voted

for the upper classes. (That situation hasn't changed much.
Some politicians today may pledge anything to get elected
but fail to keep their promises later on.)

The Romans, like other ancient peoples, had no written
laws, so when a man went to trial, he had to depend on the
priests who had committed the law to memory. The accused
man never was sure whether he had received justice, because
he didn't know the law.

The Senate decided to correct this in 451 B.C., when ten
men were appointed to collect the laws and put them in
writing. The ten worked hard to produce a complete body of
law that would satisfy the Roman people. They even sent a
delegation to Athens to study the Greek laws, the most important of which were those that had to do with business.
They faithfully recorded the many laws entrusted to the
memories of the priests.

At the end of their term—about a year and a half—they had
completed twelve chapters of laws that were—and still are—
known as the Code of the Twelve Tables. This document is
as highly prized among the Italians of today as the Magna
Charta (which we shall hear about later) is among English-
speaking nations.

The Code of the Twelve Tables named many rights: the
right to vote, the right to become a priest, the right to own
property, the right to make contracts and have them enforced, and the right to file lawsuits to remedy any wrongs
and have them tried in court. There was also the right to
contract a marriage, a right until then exercised only by the
head of the family, who arranged for marriages without regard for the feelings of participants; and the right to be
divorced if the marriage didn't work out.

A new position, that of judge, was created; both the magistrate and the judge were officials of the court. There was no jury. The magistrate read the law that applied to the case and instructed the judge, who then decided the case in favor of one or the other in a lawsuit.

In actual practice, the magistrates made more laws than the Assembly or the Senate, and it was done this way:

A magistrate might have a case that was not covered in detail in the law. He would have to find some broad rule that applied to that case, then decide on an extension of the law so that it would serve the purpose. In so doing, he set a precedent—a rule that could be followed by other magistrates in similar cases in the future.

In case after case, the magistrate had to write his own law because the specific situation wasn't covered in the written law. When other magistrates accepted his version, the rulings became law.

Precedents—that is, similar cases that have happened before and have been decided in a certain way—are widely used in legal practice today. Nearly always, a good lawyer today can cite a number of precedents to bolster the arguments in his own case. And nearly always these have great weight with the judge.

Today, when a judge can find only a broad principle to guide him, he may have a decision that will set a precedent and, in time, this will have the effect of law.

In the days of the Roman Republic, many of the magistrates had no legal training and little knowledge of the laws. But there were others who had studied the law and who could advise the magistrates who, in turn, instructed the judges. These lawyers who helped guide the magistrates also made many laws by the precedent method. For example:

If there was a new decision on law to be made and the magistrate was not capable of making it, he would ask a lawyer, who would tell him how to interpret that particular law—thus creating a new law.

In other instances, wise men with great reputations could go to a magistrate and tell him that certain cases required certain interpretations. Very often, the magistrate was afraid to oppose the wise men because they were better known than he, so the wise lawyers, through this method, created many new laws.

These "experts" were known as jurists—men learned in the science of law—and there was plenty of room for them. The written laws were no more than a framework on which the jurists could build.

Both the Roman people and the jurists took their laws seriously and they were eager to put more solid substance, well distributed, on the framework. When the body of the law showed signs of bulging in one place or being too thin in another, something was wrong. The jurists and the law professors tried to find the source of the trouble and make changes.

Through these methods, the Romans became scientists in the law, and the amount of new laws they produced was unequaled until the twentieth century. They studied countless human problems and tried to find remedies for them in their laws. These became the foundation of the English common law, which is the basis of many court decisions today.

Numerous brilliant lawyers in Rome received their training from these learned jurists, but the greatest perhaps was Cicero. In his time, the first century B.C., the most effective man at a trial was the lawyer who could give the best oration. Cicero soon became famous as an orator, and some of the trials in which he participated were so popular with the citizens that they were moved to the Roman Forum.

Thousands of people crowded in there to listen to Cicero's voice. After he had won two important cases, which assured his fame, he went to Greece, where he studied the works of the great Athenian philosophers.

After Cicero returned to Rome, he ran for office and was elected a magistrate, then a consul. When Catiline was accused of a plot against the state, Cicero represented the government and his orations against Catiline and others quickly destroyed the conspiracy. If you have studied Latin in high school, undoubtedly you are familiar with Cicero's writings.

As a jurist, Cicero wrote many theories of law that have had a great effect on legal thinking through the centuries. His readers were urged to think more positively and to lean less on what had happened in the past and what had been accepted as natural laws.

In legal agreements and contracts, there often was confusion as to the exact meaning of certain phrasing, just as there is today. Cicero usually approached the problem by asking a question: "What was the intention of these people when they made the agreement?" If that could be answered, perhaps through proof offered by witnesses, then it would be easier to interpret the sometimes obscure wording of a contract.

The intent of a man's acts was brought into criminal cases by Cicero, too. For centuries, the criminal laws had been strictly enforced to the letter, with no room for other circumstances. For example, if a man on horseback ran down and killed another, was he guilty of murder? If it could be proved that he had been riding the horse when it ran down and killed the other man, he could be accused and convicted.

But Cicero injected a new line of reasoning: Did the rider intend to have his horse run over the other man? Was the horse a runaway, out of the control of the rider? Was the death an accident? Cicero's theory, which eventually became law, was that a man should be punished according to the intent of his actions rather than for the actions themselves.

In still another way, Cicero was responsible for softening the law. Let's suppose the man on horseback rode through another man's field, trampled and ruined a good share of his crop. Did he intend to do this? Or was it case of not being able to control his horse?

Before Cicero's time, intent had nothing to do with it. The guilty man had to pay for the damages and could be punished, too.

But under Cicero's reasoning, if the horseback rider had not intended to do any damage to the crop, he couldn't be punished like a criminal. But as the owner of the horse, he was responsible for what the horse did, so he could be forced to pay the damages.

That is the situation as it is today.

During this period, Julius Caesar had gained control of the Roman government, but he was striving for a democracy. He was opposed by another strong leader, Mark Antony. After Caesar's death, his adopted son, Octavian, took up the fight and defeated Antony.

The Senate approved of Octavian and bestowed many powers upon him. He became an emperor and the Senate gave him the name Augustus. Rome had gained control of many lands through conquest, and Augustus became the most powerful ruler in the civilized world outside the Orient.

But he did not abuse his great power. He tried to carry on the principles of democracy, even though he ruled an empire.

By this time, interest in the law had become so great that many men were giving opinions and some of them conflicted. Augustus realized that there were too many laws and too many jurists who had power to influence the courts. While much of the law they had created was good, a great deal of it was bad. There was a threat of rebellion and the danger of anarchy—that is, rule by lawless mobs.

To make the laws clearer and more effective, Augustus ruled that the jurists no longer could advise the courts. Then he carefully selected three of the best jurists, gave them imperial power, and they acted as advisers to the magistrates.

As a result, some of the bad laws were thrown out. The others were put in force in all courts. This had the effect of restoring order, but it slowed down the development of new ideas in the law. Augustus felt this was necessary to keep down the threat of anarchy. He was right; he saved Rome from that fate.

Augustus was succeeded by three emperors who had few of his good points and many traits that were bad. Perhaps the worst was Nero, who could be designated the original playboy. In A.D. 68, he was thrown out by the army and a new line of Roman emperors began.

One of the best of these was Hadrian, who undertook something no other Roman ruler had done before. A vast and active genius, he spent five years touring Gaul, Spain, England, Mauretania, Greece, Sicily and other provinces. He

stayed in each long enough to learn something about the
people, their customs and their laws. Many of the local laws
that he liked were copied and carried back to Rome, to be
added to those governing the entire empire.

He discovered that one of the greatest needs was communication. A mail service of sorts existed in some provinces,
but it was a haphazard courier service at best. On his return
to Rome, Hadrian created a national postal service.

But he didn't stay in Rome long. Soon he was off to Africa,
to see how other peoples lived. He visited Greece again, went
to Syria and Palestine, took a trip to Egypt.

Having spent much time talking to the people and study-
ing their laws, Hadrian returned to Rome and devoted a
great deal of his energy to improving the Roman laws. As
the emperor, he was the Roman Supreme Court, but there
were many lower courts. As often as he could, Hadrian sat in
as magistrate and almost always, he interpreted the laws in
favor of the lowly or "underdog."

Hadrian's greatest contribution to the growth of the law
was in the field of equity. In simple terms, equity is a body
of legal rules designed to supplement or override any laws
that are too technical, too narrow or rigid, so that fairness
will prevail within reasonable limits.

In Rome, then the center of all culture and education, there
were many foreigners, and more came in every day. They
could not vote, they could not file lawsuits under Roman law.
But problems were constantly arising and something had to
be done.

A new magistrate was appointed and a new court was set
up to handle cases in which aliens were involved. Since there
were no specific laws dealing with aliens, the magistrates

leaned heavily on equity or what they considered fair treatment. To do this, a magistrate had to find an existing law that broadly applied to the case, then stretch it to fit the particular circumstances.

Because of no strict rules or formalities, this led to the development of what was known as the formula. This was the informal way of getting cases before judges. The magistrate would study a case, assign it to a judge and write out the formula of what the judge was to find if he determined certain facts to be true.

This informal method became so popular that, eventually, the magistrates were allowed to apply the formula to cases involving Roman citizens, too. In time, equity, which originally was the basis of the judgments applying to aliens, was merged with the Roman law.

Again, as judges relied more and more on educated jurists to give interpretations, new laws were made. The quantity of these became so huge that Hadrian appointed a commission to simplify and consolidate all the laws. The head of this commission was Julian, who had been a special aide to Hadrian.

Julian and the other commissioners studied each law, each precedent, each decision rendered by a judge and based on an opinion by a jurist. As a result of their work, Roman law was consolidated into what was called the Perpetual Edict, which was thought to include every possible situation. It was expected that the Perpetual Edict would put an end to the growth of equity, but it didn't.

Jurists continued to give opinions that were incorporated into the law. This continued until about A.D. 225, when Emperor Alexander Severus put a stop to it. After that, in Roman

law, all rules were made by decree of the emperor or those
working under his direction.

But there are many points of medieval Roman laws at
which those interested in the legal profession particularly
should have a look. For example, the laws relating to torts
were highly developed by the Roman jurists. A tort is any
sort of wrongful action (except breach of contract) for which
a civil suit may be brought.

If a man became angry at another and beat him so that
he suffered painful wounds, he could be taken to court and
forced to pay. But he didn't pay because of the pain the
other man had suffered; he paid because the other had lost
dignity.

The injury to a person's dignity actually was the basis for
most of the penalties imposed by the courts against offenders.

A trespass was a tort. A man on horseback might gallop
through a field and destroy a great deal of grain. He would
have to pay—and again, the reason was that the owner of
the field had suffered loss of dignity.

There were several forms of negligence in the Roman laws.
One was ordinary negligence. For example, a man plowing
a field might come across a large stone that he wanted to
dispose of. If he threw it and hit someone who was passing,
the passer-by could collect damages.

But that same incident might not be as serious if the
charge were contributory negligence. Suppose there were
many rocks in the field and the passer-by knew they were
thrown out frequently. If he went by the field without watching, he might be charged with contributory negligence and
could not collect as much, since it was partly his fault for
being careless.

Gross negligence and minor negligence also called for varied penalties. For example:

A farmer is using a scythe with a very sharp blade to cut weeds from his garden. He finishes his work and leans the handle of the scythe against a tree with a sharp blade across a path regularly used by people on foot. After nightfall, it is hard to see in the darkness. (There were no street lights in those days.) A passer-by steps on the sharp blade and seriously cuts his foot.

The man who left the scythe where it would endanger another is guilty of gross negligence.

But let us suppose that he laid it flat on the ground, outside the usual path or walkway. A curious child might come along and cut his finger by touching the blade.

The owner of the scythe then would be guilty of minor negligence.

There were other types of torts that came to be known as unlawful actions, for which there were penalties.

The Romans took many of their trade or business laws from those of the Jews and the Greeks and added some of their own. At the peak of greatness of the Roman Empire, there was much commerce in the city of Rome, as well as in the provinces. Laws of commerce were essential.

Many Roman contracts in the Middle Ages were quite simple: A man promised something and another man accepted his promise. Unlike the contract of today, there was no need for a "consideration" to make a contract binding. It was generally believed in those days that, if a person promised to do something, he would do it.

Although there were many wealthy men and powerful organizations in the business life of medieval Rome, there were no corporations as they exist today. But there were syndicates that sold shares. And some wealthy men held shares in numerous enterprises.

In addition to retail business, there was a great deal of international trade. A syndicate would control a ship or a fleet of ships and employ the men who sailed them and handled the cargo.

Then, as today, any large venture had to be financed—that is, backed by borrowed money. This promoted the rise of private banks, run by men of great wealth. As the demand for money grew, bankers got together and formed banking syndicates. This was necessary when some venture was too big or too risky for one banker.

For example, a commercial group might want to outfit a fleet of ships to sail to a foreign port and bring back goods not usually available in Rome, which would bring a good price if they could be offered for sale in the local shops. Not wanting to risk so much money—or not having enough—a banker would approach others and they would band together to share the gamble and the interest the money would bring if the venture were successful.

In the beginning, the interest rate was 12 per cent. But the Emperor Justinian thought this was too high for most purposes and stepped in with legal limits. The bankers still could charge 12 per cent for the more hazardous ventures, but if a man wanted to go into a stable type of business, where there was not much risk, the banker could charge him no more than 4 per cent.

Justinian fixed other rates, ranging from 4 to 12 per cent, but, in time, an average rate of 6 per cent became common, just as it is today.

Also, as happens today, some businesses failed. The Roman laws permitted a man to have his debts erased through bankruptcy, but there was so much disgrace attached to it that no man would take bankruptcy action unless he was forced to do so.

The laws provided that a man could voluntarily go into bankruptcy and have the slate wiped clean of debts. But anyone who did this was deprived by law of many of his rights as a citizen. He was regarded as a man who couldn't be trusted. It was unlikely that he ever again would be able to borrow money, to go into business or to regain his former social position in the community.

This differs in some ways from our modern laws. A man who goes through bankruptcy loses none of his legal rights. There may be a tendency on the part of his creditors not to trust him if he starts a new business, but there is no law to prevent a fresh start.

It should be added that there have been countless instances of men who failed in one business and had their debts wiped out, who later made good in other ventures and paid off all the debt that had been forgiven in the first venture.

The Roman laws devised several types of wills by which the owner of property could specify who should receive it. Then, as now, the wife was entitled to a part, as were the sons. Daughters had no legal status as heirs. (A wife's legal share of an estate is known as her dower right.) One kind of will required seven witnesses. Each had to affix his signature after the document was signed by the maker and also had to sign on the outside after it was sealed.

A simplified type of will was one drawn up by a soldier

who was away on a military campaign, with the witnesses as fellow warriors. One witness usually sufficed.

The third type was one that was drawn up by the maker (known as the testator) in his own handwriting. As forms of "wills" became standardized, legal guidance diminished in importance. Today, banks and trust companies suggest but do not draft wills. That would be the corporate practice of law and is forbidden by statutory and judicial prohibitions.

Many testators lived long after their wills had been drawn, and most wanted to make changes. The law provided this could be done by attaching a codicil—an addition to a will. Some testators named administrators in the codicils and specified that certain heirs would receive the income from certain property. This was the beginning of trusts, which are in wide use today by wealthy people who want to make sure that certain persons benefit from their estates.

Meanwhile, the profession of the lawyer had become well established. There were two great law schools—one at Byzantium, the other at Beirut—as well as many lesser ones. The professors were plagued by the great amount of laws that had accumulated through legislation, through precedent, and through opinions by learned jurists.

Emperor Justinian realized this and set up a commission to consolidate and condense the laws into one work (a series of volumes) and to produce a legal textbook. The great work was completed in 533 and the textbook was published the same year. (It should be remembered that printing had not yet been invented and that all books were laboriously written by hand.)

Justinian's legal works continued to exist long after his

death. Following the invention of the printing press and movable type about 1440, most of the emperor's books were printed. They have served ever since as source material for legal scholars, jurists and lawmakers.

# 5. The Germans and the Franks

One of the main contributions of the Germans to the well-being of mankind was the belief in freedom, from the earliest times. The ancient Germans met in open-air assemblies to vote on government policy, to elect officials and judges. Trials were held in these open assemblies and punishments usually were fairly fixed according to the seriousness of the offense.

Even after the conquests of Charlemagne, who was crowned as the Emperor of the Holy Roman Empire by Pope Leo III in 800, the open-air courts continued. Charlemagne did not try to stop them, but he set up a higher court to supervise what they were doing. He selected men learned in the laws to visit the provinces and sit in at the trials, to make sure that justice was done. These men consulted with the judges in rendering decisions and actually were the forerunners of our present-day jury.

After Charlemagne's death, there was not a strong ruler, and many separate bodies sprang up. A man who held a great deal of property and owned a mansion with many slaves became the power in a given area—and the smaller landowners about him grew afraid. They made deals with the lord of the manor to give up their holdings and work for him in return for protection from outside invaders.

This was the beginning of the feudal system. There were only two classes of people at first—serfs and lords. The serfs tilled the soil and did other work or acted as vassals. A vassal had to go along with his lord if he went into battle. Both might ride horses, but if the master's mount were killed, the vassal had to give up his horse to his lord.

If the invading force were large, the male members of the master's family, dressed in armor, rode against the attackers, while a group of serfs fought on foot. The only advantage in life for the serf was that he had a home and food and a promise that his security would be defended.

Each feudal lord held court to deal with violators of the laws, most of which had been made by the master himself. His judgment was final.

For a time, the feudal system was a complete setback for the progress of mankind. But a new class gradually developed. These were tradesmen, merchants and artisans—men who made and sold things that even the lord of the manor needed, such as plates, pots, kettles, knives, and the like.

Villages were established and they grew into towns. The middle class formed guilds that, in time, were more powerful than the forces of the feudal lord.

With these developments, some of the old customs were restored. Court was held either in the open air or in rooms

with one end open. This was a return to the freedom of the
old public trials, but some features were different. No trial
could begin before sunrise or last beyond sunset. Nor could
any trial last more than one day.

The greatest difference, however, was in the trial by ordeal.
It was believed that God would determine whether a man
was guilty or innocent. He might be thrown into a body of
deep water. If the water rejected him—that is, if he managed to come out alive instead of drowning—it was the judgment of the court that God had found him not guilty.

There were many other forms of trial by ordeal. An accused man would carry a red-hot iron nine feet. Then his
hand would be bandaged for three days. If there was no
blood when the bandage was removed, he was freed. If his
hand was bloody, he was considered guilty.

But sweeping legal changes were ahead.

Many serfs decided they could do better as craftsmen.
They bought their freedom from the feudal barons and
moved into the towns. As the towns grew, trade between
them flourished and there was need for business law.

The towns were organized, with councils that passed ordinances, or local laws. In addition to the presiding judge of the
court, lay judges were appointed and they heard the cases with
the presiding judge. He had to consult them before he could
give his decision and could not render it unless all agreed.
This was a further step in the direction of a jury system.

The growth of the towns and the loss of serfs brought an
end to the feudal system. Roman laws were revived and there
was a renewed interest in reading and writing—arts that had,
for a few centuries, been lost to most people, being kept
alive only by the Church.

# 6. The Laws of the Church

Before the Roman laws were written (and before the Christian era), the priests of the pagan religions were the custodians of the law. When the statutes were put in writing, the priests continued in their role of trustees.

With the beginning of the Christian Church, it was but natural that the priests should consider themselves as guardians of the laws. But the emperors and civil authorities did not agree with this in full.

Nevertheless, the Christian Church councils passed laws, both civil and religious, which they called canons, and these were put into effect as soon as they were approved by the Pope. Most of the civil laws of the Church were very much like those enacted by the legislators or jurists. In one respect, however, the canons of the Church differed from the laws made by civil authorities. They decreed that the same kind of justice was to be given every man, regardless of his position, while the civil laws had different rules for different classes of people.

St. Augustine voiced a credo in the fifth century that
Church law should be supreme, even though there was a
place for civil authority and government. It was his conten-
tion that all actions of all courts should be subject to the final
authority of the Church.

For centuries there was conflict between the civil rulers
and the Church as to which would be boss. Christianity had
become the official, compulsory religion of the Roman Empire
and many of the citizens took their cases to the priests rather
than to the civil judges. But the emperors were not always
willing to take orders from the Pope, who was the head of
the Church.

The Pope's claims were based on the belief that the mantle
of Jesus Christ had been passed on to the Popes by St. Peter
and that the Pope was, in fact, the direct representative of
God.

The first to accept this concept was Charlemagne, after
the Church had crowned him Emperor of the Holy Roman
Empire. He was allowed to reign and administer the affairs
of his vast realm, but he always was subject to the Church.
This worked out well enough until after Charlemagne's death.

The rise of feudalism meant the decline of culture and
such arts as reading and writing. During the feudal period,
often called the Dark Ages, the priests of the Church were
the only people who could read and write. They preserved
Roman law, but they also did some altering of it, making the
civil laws fit into a religious base. However, the Church,
through courts set up in all the provinces, took a great step
in the direction of human justice. For centuries, one man
could accuse another and the latter would be prosecuted.
The Church changed that, requiring that the accused be

prosecuted only by a public prosecutor after sufficient evidence had been produced to warrant a trial. This eliminated a great number of cases that were instigated by nothing more than spite or personal vengeance.

The Church courts also eliminated the primitive practice of trial by ordeal. It substituted a system that is similar in some respects to the practices of today. A pleading—that is, a statement to the judge—had to be in writing. Both sides in a dispute could be represented by counsel and either side could have the testimony of witnesses. Even written evidence could be introduced by either side.

St. Thomas Aquinas, who lived in the thirteenth century, probably was the greatest of the Church philosophers. One of his basic rules was that "the kingdom does not exist for the king, but the king for the kingdom." Aquinas spread the theory of natural law and laid down a rule. He said that natural law was founded on "right reason." The Church adopted this idea because it contended that all laws were those of God.

It was the claim of the Church that there was something higher than man-made laws. This is a creed that has continued to this day, although the influence of the Church waned in the courts and, in time, the Church itself ceased to claim that it had power over the states.

# 7. The Europeans and Continental Law

With the spread of feudalism in the ninth century, most of Europe was overrun by hordes of barbarians. Although they accepted the Christian religion, they knew nothing of culture and cared less for it. Most of the conquered people were drawn down to their level and, as a result, the great law schools faded and died.

But there was a small group of literate people whose culture was not quite wiped out. They continued to study, to seek learning, mostly with the help of the monks in the monasteries. They studied law, but it was on a rather haphazard basis.

When the feudal system began to decline in the twelfth century, new universities were established, first in Italy, later in other countries of Western Europe.

Even though many historical documents had been destroyed, the Codes of Justinian and his textbook for law students had been saved. During the next two centuries, many universities for the study of law sprang up in Europe. The principles of Justinian were taught, but they were not applied to current problems.

About the middle of the fourteenth century, during the reign of Charles IV, a brilliant professor named Bartolus, who was teaching law in France at the age of twenty-six, began to apply the laws of Justinian to everyday events. This practical approach spread to other schools which emerged from the Dark Ages sparked with great zeal.

Started originally as law schools or universities, they gradually added other subjects, until many became general universities. They awarded the three degrees that are familiar to us today. The lowest was Bachelor of Laws or of Arts or whatever subject the student majored in at the university. The next was a Master's and the third was a Doctor's degree.

Bartolus became an authority on the law and his works were widely used, especially after the invention of printing, nearly a century following his death, made it possible to print and distribute many copies of the same books.

A basic legal principle first stated by Bartolus is in effect today: When there is a violation of a law, the offender is to be tried under the laws of the place where the violation occurred. Or if there is a dispute over a contract, the laws of the place where the contract was drawn will apply. For example, if a man commits a traffic violation while he is driving through Pennsylvania, he cannot be tried under the laws of New York State, even though he may live in New York. Or if the New Yorker made a contract in Pennsylvania, he would have to abide by the laws of that state, and could not operate under the laws of New York, which might be different.

Fifty-two years before America was discovered, the print-

ing press and movable type were invented. By the time
Columbus made his famous voyage, there were many printing presses in Europe turning out books. Writing was stimulated and men put their thoughts into books. For the first
time in the known history of humanity, large numbers of men
began to think for themselves. They revolted against laws
they didn't consider right and religious practices in which
they didn't believe.

The most famous of these was Martin Luther. He studied
law for a while, then decided to become a priest. But he
didn't agree with the rituals and dogma of the Roman
Catholic Church and began the Protestant movement. Luther placed personal liberty above everything else and insisted that freedom of religious thought was every man's
right. Any man could read the Bible and interpret it for
himself, he said, also, no man should be forced to accept an
interpretation of the Bible by any other man, or any group of
men. Luther's doctrine was adopted by many others, who
left the Roman Catholic Church.

Another man, John Calvin, also revolted against the
Roman Catholic Church, but he was entirely different from
Luther. Calvin insisted on a strict interpretation of the Bible.
He was an advocate of what we call "the letter of the law"
(as opposed to the spirit of the law). He was stern and un-
yielding in his views. He, too, found many followers.

The creeds of both men were debated in the colonies then
forming in America. Both of them were to have great influence in the future struggles in the new world.

Twenty-one years after Columbus discovered America, an
an Italian law student named Andrea Alciati wrote a book
on Justinian law and announced that it was time some

changes were made in it. He became a professor of law at an Italian university, and later went to France.

Alciati had a faculty for making even a dull subject seem interesting. Students vied with each other to attend his lectures. He had studied the laws of all lands, but he found those of the Romans by far the best. There were good points in the other laws, too, though. What the world needed, he said, was to take the Roman laws and improve upon them.

So popular was Alciati that he drew many famous people to his lectures, including the French royal family, Sir Thomas More, even John Calvin. Although he didn't agree with all the dogma and rituals of the Church, Alciati remained a Catholic.

Alciati started the legal minds of Europe on new trains of thought. They soon agreed that he was right when he said there was much room for improvements in the laws. Both students and professors brought out new ideas on the subject. These were passed around to classes in the universities in different lands and often were debated. For the first time in history, independent thinking by great numbers of men was encouraged. This was a period when new ideas spread rapidly through the world, which now included a few struggling colonies in North and South America. It was almost as if mankind were trying to make up for the time it had lost during the Dark Ages when literacy was almost erased.

The greatest legal mind of the sixteenth century was a Frenchman, Jacques Cujas, who had learned law from a student of Alciati. At the age of twenty-seven, Cujas established his own law school. Later, he accepted posts at various other universities. But wherever he went, he always had a large following of students. He had a great desire to learn

and he built a great library in his home, in which he collected over 400 historical documents, mostly manuscripts
produced by scholars of the past.

Anybody who was interested could come to Cujas' study
to read his books and manuscripts. Some worthy students
were taken into his home and allowed to live there until they
had finished their legal training. On many occasions, Cujas
even loaned money to his students.

He studied the existing laws and went back to the roots
of them when he could find material produced in an earlier
age. He never hesitated to make his ideas known. Some of
them conflicted with the popular beliefs, and he engaged in
many arguments. Whether he won or lost in these, he was
highly respected throughout Europe. His main contribution
was his collection of documents which were of invaluable
help to later students of the law and its history.

Five European philosophers of the seventeenth and eighteenth centuries urged major changes that helped the law to
grow. Much could be said about each, but there is not enough
space here for that. We shall have to be satisfied to state
briefly who they were and the contribution each made:

Gottfried Wilhelm von Leibnitz was a German philosopher
and statesman who believed that the same laws for the whole
world might lessen our troubles. To achieve this, we would
need a universal religion, a universal language and method
of writing, universal system of weights and measures, the
same kind of money throughout the world. It is a goal that
various men have been striving for ever since.

Baron Montesquieu was a French nobleman and jurist who
gave up politics to write books. The most notable of these
was *The Spirit of Laws,* which was said to have been the

most widely read by the members of the United States Constitutional Convention. Montesquieu insisted that there should be three branches of government: the executive, the legislative and the judicial. This principle was adopted by the framers of the United States Constitution.

Voltaire was the penname of a French writer who, through satire and criticism, made government officials realize their weaknesses. His great gift to the development of the law was that he caused lawmakers to think, to study the statutes and try to find ways to improve them. Voltaire held up a mirror that reflected men as they were and laid bare their shortcomings.

Jean Jacques Rousseau ran away from home when he was a youth, led the life of an adventurer for several years and finally settled in Paris to write. His most important work, *The Social Contract,* voiced two principles that became part of the American revolt against the British: That government should exist only with the consent of the governed and that all men are created equal. (Thomas Jefferson changed this to "all men are created free and equal.")

The Marquis di Beccaria was an Italian nobleman who took a particular interest in criminal law. He was horrified by many of the cruel punishments and by the filth in European jails and prisons. He wrote a book, *An Essay on Crimes and Punishments,* in which he criticized many of the penalties, asserting that the punishment should be no more serious than the crime. Beccaria was the first to denounce punishment for vengeance and to suggest that society would be better off if men could be restored to usefulness, instead of putting them in dungeons to rot. He also urged that capital punishment be abolished. The death penalty still is given for many serious crimes in some states and in some countries. But there is a strong movement to do away with it in more and more nations.

Becarria's book was translated into French and English and had a wide circulation. It started a reform that is still going on. In particular, it influenced the men who wrote the first ten amendments to the United States Constitution to prohibit "cruel and unusual punishments."

# 8. Napoleon's Civil Codes and Criminal Procedure

In spite of the widespread interest in the law and the many wise men with new ideas, the laws in Continental Europe still were a great mass of conflicting statutes when Napoleon Bonaparte came to power in France.

Napoleon is best known as a general, as a ruler who led armies into many battles, as a dictator who tried to conquer Europe, as a man who dreamed of ruling the world. He was not a lawyer, but he soon realized the need to bring some uniformity into the many existing laws. He appointed the best legal minds of France to do the actual work, but he didn't let the problem rest there. He often sat in at meetings of the commission and held many discussions with the men who were wading through the welter of laws. His lack of legal training did not stop him from making suggestions based on reason, logic or common sense. He did not impose his will on the commission, but the men he had appointed did accept his ideas when they were good.

The final decisions were printed in several volumes, the whole known as the *Codes of Napoleon.* The unified French laws were so much simpler and more usable for the whole country that they soon spread to most of Continental Europe.

Here is an example of the difference that the Code made. Previously a man could travel a hundred miles across France and find five different laws to cover the same act or offense, but, after the commission had unified the laws, only one law governed that offense. Something of this sort had been needed in Europe since the end of feudalism. Eventually, most other nations drew up their own unified laws, but they were based on Napoleon's Codes.

Napoleon himself realized that his defeat at the Battle of Waterloo would erase the memory of many victorious battles. "But," he added, "what will live eternally is my Civil Code."

# 9. The English Laws

Since the English legal system was the foundation of law in the United States and Canada, it is important that we take a good look at the growth of the English laws.

England was settled by peoples from many lands. Some were invaders, others were fleeing from invaders. They had clan laws, but we know little about them. Our first such record is of the Celts, who fled across the Channel to England when their homeland was invaded by Julius Caesar, about 50 B.C. The Celts kept going until they landed in Ireland, where they settled. Like other primitive peoples, their laws had not been put in writing, but were entrusted to the priests, who handed them down from one generation to another.

The Celtic priests were known as the Druids, and each was a judge. Any legal action, whether criminal or civil, was taken before a Druid. He decided whether a man was guilty of a crime and fixed penalties, or he settled disputes, such as those over the possession of land or sheep.

As the population grew, Ireland was divided into five districts, each ruled by a king, with a chief king who had authority over the other five. An assembly known as the Dal began meeting to debate the affairs of the people and the government. (From this grew the present Irish Parliament, the Dail.)

St. Patrick is known chiefly as the man who brought Christianity to Ireland. He also was a great jurist. Through his efforts, a commission collected and revised the Irish laws into a work known as the *Code of Patrick*. These laws had a religious base, but they called for settling legal matters in public courts run by judges known as brehons.

Patrick's efforts to create peace among neighbors did not always work. The Irish temper was such that many a quarrel was still settled by fists.

During the next 400 years, the Irish were the most literate people in the world and their legal scholars, with the help of the priests, wrote many brilliant volumes on the law.

In an age that was abandoning culture, the Irish continued to promote learning. They sent missionaries to England to teach the Anglo-Saxons how to read and write.

England had been invaded by the Romans, the Angles and the Saxons, the Germans and the Danes. Each of these peoples had brought some of their own laws, which were written in German. The most notable was that trait developed in the open-air assemblies in the German forests—the strong love for personal freedom.

The English legal system developed slowly. Families were divided into hundreds and each such group had its own judge for minor cases. Every hundred group sent delegates to the county courts, which were set up to try the more serious offenses and disputes.

This system was in use when Howell the Good became king of South Wales in the tenth century. Howell took a great interest in the laws and tried to develop them along just lines. He noted that many people were deprived of the services of the courts because they had to work all day. He ordered his chief justices to hold court at night for anybody who couldn't be there in the daytime.

Feudalism, which was the main form of government in Europe, spread to England, but it did not gain the stranglehold it had on the Continent.

Many families elected to join a lord or baron and become a part of his little kingdom, in return for protection, mainly against invaders from other regions. They were subject to the laws of the barony and had to submit to trials in the baronial courts, with the baron himself making all the decisions because he acted as judge.

But other English families chose to remain free of the feudal lords. The hundreds system of local courts continued and each hundred group sent representatives to act as judges in the county courts. The head judge of a county court had to be one who could read law books, and usually this was a priest.

When William the Conqueror invaded England with his band of Normans and Frenchmen, he won the loyalty of the feudal barons by promising he wouldn't change their domains. Thus assured that he had control of his realm, he removed the clergymen who had been county judges and put in his own men to preside at the county courts.

Although William and other rulers made some changes in

the laws, Henry II, who reigned about a century after the Norman conquest, really began the English system of law that exists today. He appointed a large number of circuit judges, who rode to all the counties and held court.

The people were not forced to go to the national courts, but many did. They seemed to feel that they would get a fairer deal from a judge appointed by the king. Those who wished, however, still could take their disputes to the county courts.

In England, as in other countries throughout the world at that time, there was no national law that applied equally to all people in all counties. Instead, there was a great number of local laws and some of them differed quite drastically. The national judges began applying the same law—often laws that did not actually exist or interpretations of laws to suit the situation—to all sections of the country, and the common law began to grow.

The writ—a paper on which there was writing—came into use by the king's courts. Originally, a writ was an order to start a legal action, bearing the seal of the king.

Henry believed it was desirable to have most important cases tried in the national courts, but he did not want to tell the people they had to take their legal actions to the king's courts. However, he found a way to do this without the actual order. Any offense, civil or criminal, was a case for the national court if it involved violation of the king's peace. Somebody discovered that almost any serious offense could be said to have been a breach of the king's peace. This was put into the writs and more and more of the cases went to the national courts.

Henry started another reform that is still with us. If a man was accused of a crime, he could not be forced to go to trial until he had been indicted. The sheriff, the county's chief officer of the law, appointed twelve men to act as a grand jury. The facts of an accusation were taken to the grand jury, and if they agreed, there was cause for the man to stand trial and he was indicted.

Another jury came into existence at the trial. This was known as the petit jury, just as it is today. But the work of the twelve jurors in those days was quite different from that of our jurors today. Each of the twelve men had to find out the facts related to the crime for himself. He could go around and ask questions of anyone; he could listen to the lawyers, or he could just draw his own conclusions.

At the trial, the jurors were the witnesses. Each told what he had learned or concluded. Actual witnesses to the crime could not be heard in court; they could only tell their stories to the jurors outside the court.

All twelve of the jurors had to agree on the guilt or innocence of the accused; otherwise there was no verdict. If they couldn't agree, they were dismissed and twelve more jurors were appointed. This went on until there was a jury that did agree.

For more than a hundred years, the use of the writ as an instrument of legal action had multiplied. There were so many different kinds of writs that even the best lawyers couldn't keep up with them.

At the time when Henry II died and was succeeded on the English throne by Richard the Lion-hearted, the Chief Justice of England was Ranulf de Glanville, a brilliant man and a great jurist. Toward the end of the twelfth century, De Glanville wrote a book to guide lawyers and judges; it described every writ that had been devised and how it was to be used.

The growth of the writ system meant that the old, primitive methods were vanishing, that the law now was basing its cases on facts and the testimony of at least a dozen lawful witnesses (the jurors) who gave their statements under oath.

Richard was succeeded by his brother John, who became one of the most hated English kings. He was cruel and unjust and his taxes were so high that they created an impossible burden.

The barons got together and revolted. They drew up a long document they called the Magna Charta and demanded a meeting with King John. He met the barons at Runnymede, in 1215, and soon realized that he was in danger of losing not only his throne but his life. Therefore he signed the Magna Charta, which often has been called the cornerstone of liberty. There were dozens of clauses, each granting his subjects some sort of privilege. For example, the right of trial by a jury of his peers was assured every free man. Nearly every principle of the Charta was for the good of free men.

There were relatively few free men at that time. Most were barons, lords, knights and a few prominent men of the towns. Most other men—the great majority—still were serfs, who were no more than slaves to the land.

But the principles were there and they applied to any free man. With the passage of each century, more men became free and could claim the liberty granted them as such by the Magna Charta.

Not every king after John recognized the Magna Charta; some ignored it. But others accepted it as a basic set of rules and abided by them. It was not until early in the seventeenth century that the Magna Charta finally became one of the key parts of the British Constitution.

But there was one phase of law that was growing steadily. This was the common law. If a case came before a judge and he could find no specific statute covering that situation, he gave a decision based on his own reasoning of what the law would have provided, if there had been one.

The next time that situation came to the attention of a judge, he would be guided by the decision of the judge in the prior case. Thus, the law became common, even though it never had been written as a statute.

There were many cases of this kind, not covered by legislation, and they grew into what is now a great body of common law. The rules by which they are decided are not different from what they were centuries ago—except in those situations that have been altered by legislation.

When Edward I became King of England, near the end of the thirteenth century, he immediately hailed the Magna Charta and vowed that he would abide by its principles. In addition, Edward went much farther. Prior to his reign, there had been a parliament, but its members were barons who had little interest in the common welfare. Also, its members had no power. They could debate and propose new statutes, but could not enact them into law. Only the king could do that; and up to the time of Edward, most kings had ignored the advice of Parliament more often than they accepted it.

Edward apparently had a real desire for more rule by the people. He reorganized Parliament and added commoners—two knights from every shire and two burgesses from every town. (A knight is a man with a title two ranks below a baron. A shire is now known officially in England as a county. A burgess was a prominent citizen.)

The new Parliament, in which the barons were outnumbered, debated and passed new laws which Edward approved. Parliament still was just one body then. About 1660, it was divided into two—the House of Lords and the House of Commons.

At that time, there were two languages in England—the German spoken by the Anglo-Saxons and the French brought to England by the Normans. Each language group had picked up words from the other. With encouragement from Edward, the two languages were merged into what became English. This was a great forward step, although many years were to pass before some degree of uniformity was achieved.

Because of the frequent disregard for the law in the remote areas of the country, Edward appointed a knight in each shire who became a justice of the peace, also a court to settle minor disputes. This setup still exists in many parts of the United States and England.

There were higher courts whose judges were barons. Some of these were willing to accept bribes. When this happened too often, there was a scandal. King Edward investigated and learned that many of the barons who were sitting as judges had no legal knowledge but had accepted appointments because they saw a chance to make easy money by selling decisions.

Edward discharged all the offending judges, as well as others who did not know the law. He made a new rule: Only a man with legal training could become a judge in the higher courts. Although a lawyer might accept a bribe, it was much more likely that he wouldn't, since honesty was a basic part of his training.

Following Edward, there were several weak kings; this permitted Parliament to grow stronger. The kings issued proclamations and orders, but Parliament passed laws and, in the end, these won out.

London grew into a great city and it became the center of learning, especially in the law. In the latter part of the sixteenth century, two men who were to have great influence on English law were born, nine years apart. One was Edward Coke, a brilliant young man who became a great lawyer; the other was Sir Francis Bacon, who not only was a great lawyer, but a philosopher and a writer whose works are still read today.

Both men vied for the same high posts, but Coke always managed to keep ahead of Bacon. Eventually, Coke was appointed Chief Justice of the Court of Common Pleas and Bacon became Attorney General.

Coke was a prudent man whose affairs usually were in order. Bacon was a spendthrift and was constantly in need of money. Coke was a champion of constitutional rights and due process of law; Bacon knew the law well enough, but he often opposed Coke.

In one such case, a proclamation of the king was the issue. The case was too complex to describe here, but the main issue was whether the king could make a law by proclamation. Bacon argued that this was a right of the king. But Coke showed that only Parliament could make a law that was binding on the people.

As a result of this, Coke was removed from office. However, he later went to Parliament, where he carried on a vigorous fight for constitutional rights. He was appointed to a commission to revise the laws. His old enemy, Bacon, was in favor of this project.

Bacon advanced to Lord Chancellor and became the king's right-hand man. But he was accused of accepting bribes, admitted his guilt and was punished. The king later reduced the penalties.

Both Coke and Bacon ended their careers doing great volumes of writing. Coke wrote on the law, Bacon on many subjects. At the time of his death, Bacon was tinkering with an idea to preserve food by refrigeration. He was a noted scientist as well as a lawyer and author.

Coke's works are valuable to lawyers and historians. Bacon's works are found on the bookshelves of many private homes and in nearly all public libraries.

About the time that Edward Coke was beginning his final tenure of public service in Parliament, a brilliant lawyer and writer, John Selden, was winning the admiration and support of other lawmakers who had been afraid to speak their minds. Selden never hesitated to oppose a proposed law that he didn't believe in, even if he had to fight the crown. Although English lawyers had been winning rights from kings ever since the signing of the Magna Charta, most members of Parliament were afraid to be openly critical of the monarch. In nearly every case, when a new right was won, it was done by persuasion or even pleading.

After Edward Coke had ruled that the king must be guided by the wishes of Parliament, there was more open debate. But many still remembered the days when the king was all-powerful and found a way to punish anyone who displeased him. Thus, there still were many members of Parliament who wouldn't come out for laws they knew to be good and just.

Nevertheless, John Selden continued to fight for more rights for the people. When he offered his Petition of Right, some timid members were fearful that he had gone too far, but one of his strongest supporters was Edward Coke, who brought more men in on Selden's side.

Two very important principles, the right of any man to go into court and challenge his imprisonment by being given the opportunity to answer the charge, and freedom of speech, were involved in the Petition of Right, drafted chiefly by Coke, a leader in the battle for constitutional rights. If, for some reason, a man was arrested and jailed unlawfully, in those days, he might be imprisoned indefinitely without a trial or without counsel to protect his rights. This was deny- ing him due process of law and it was a practice that was widespread. For example, if a commoner became involved in a dispute with a nobleman, the baron or lord could use his influence to have the commoner arrested and taken to jail, where he could be held until the nobleman saw fit to agree to his release.

The purpose of the writ of habeas corpus was to compel a jailor to produce the prisoner in court, where it could be determined whether there was legal reason for his arrest and imprisonment. If there was evidence to indicate he had com- mitted a crime, he must be indicted and given a fair trial. If there was no such evidence, then he must be freed.

The freedom of speech in the Petition of Right applied to members of Parliament who would have unlimited freedom of expression, even in matters that opposed the king.

The Petition of Right was won in the time of Charles I. Secret confinement of a prisoner, no matter with what he might be charged, was declared illegal. Freedom of speech of all members of Parliament was assured. It was only a matter of time until freedom of speech became the right of every man.

English law continued to change and it is still changing while this is being written—as everything must change with the times. In many respects, it is similar to law in the United States and Canada, which we shall discuss later.

But there is one big difference between lawyers in America and the men who practice law in England. In the latter country, if you have a case, you must take it to a solicitor, who will hear what you have to say and devise a plan of action. But he cannot carry out the action. He is required to refer it to a barrister, who will take it to court. You can't take a short cut and got to the barrister yourself. You have to go to a solicitor, who arranges for the barrister. And when you pay the bill, you remit to the solicitor. The barrister gets part of the fee, but that is a matter between him and the solicitor.

The English bar clings to a tradition that the barrister is not to be paid a fee by the client—directly. He is above all that. In this and other ways, the English are not entirely free of ancient ritual; the judges still have to wear wigs and the barristers are required to wear the ancient robes of their ancestors.

# 10. Law in America

The first document having to do with law in America was the Mayflower Compact, signed November 11, 1620, by forty-one men who had arrived at Plymouth Rock on the *Mayflower*. It was an agreement to band together into a "civil Body Politick," which would make the laws. The settlers who sailed from England on the *Mayflower* were known as Pilgrims. Other Pilgrims came to the new world and settled near Plymouth.

The Pilgrims wanted religious freedom and the right to govern themselves. They believed in democracy and tried to make it work.

But another group, the Puritans, also settled in Massachusetts, a few years later. Their number was far greater than that of the Pilgrims—and their ideas were entirely different. They set up the laws of Moses, as related in the Old Testament, as the only law of the colony. They did not try to separate civil and church affairs. They interpreted the Old Testament literally and, as a result, their laws were primitive.

The men who were chosen as leaders ruled so sternly that there were fifteen offenses for which one might be put to death. These men revived various methods of torture that had been outlawed in England and other countries. In Salem, Massachusetts, numerous women were charged with being witches and nineteen of them were put to death. In other New England colonies, it was not unusual for a man to have his ears cut off or for a woman to have a hot iron brand her tongue—with the full approval of the leaders!

During this period—the first part of the seventeenth century—the laws of England, where many individual rights had been won, were completely ignored by these settlers in the new world. But there were many persons who did not agree with the laws imposed by the Puritan rulers, and some had the courage to speak out.

One of these was Roger Williams, who had studied law. He challenged the right of the civil authorities to enforce the religious portions of the laws of Moses. When he learned that he was to be shipped back to England, he escaped and founded what is now the state of Rhode Island. He established the town of Providence and drew up its first law, the "Liberty of Conscience." By it, anyone could do as his conscience dictated, so long as he did not interfere with the rights of others. A man could belong to any church he chose—or no church at all, if that was what he wished. Rhode Island was the first colony to welcome Jews, and the synagogue built in Providence was the first in the new world.

Williams had many ideas about freedom that were popular in Rhode Island but made him hated in Massachusetts. He didn't believe in slavery and insisted that even servants were entitled to a day off every week.

Another colony whose residents believed in freedom was established near Rhode Island and it was called Connecticut. But Massachusetts, with its majority of narrow-minded leaders, continued to dominate the new world for most of the seventeenth century, despite the resistance of the Pilgrim heritage.

The cruelties under John Winthrop and his successor, John Endicott, were so horrible that they came to the attention of the English Parliament and the king. Men were put in stocks, were beaten until they were unconscious, and beaten again if they recovered their senses. It was a crime to be a Quaker— a member of the Society of Friends. Some were banished to the wilderness and many were put to death.

When William and Mary granted a new charter to Massachusetts, in 1691, church membership no longer could be required by law, and certain property rights were recognized.

But the laws of commerce imposed on the American merchants were not accepted with gratitude. American merchants were ordered to buy and sell only to England. Or if permission were granted to sell to another country, the ship carrying the cargo had to stop at an English port first, so that it could be inspected.

The passage of time and growth of the population had spread the American colonies the entire length of the Atlantic Coast. Although the English king appointed a governor for each colony, the people began electing their own local officials and every colony had its own assembly or legislature. The early settlers had not been too literate, but their descendants learned to read and write and they obtained many books from overseas.

Soon, there were printing presses in America, to produce

newspapers as well as books. One of the first authors to have his books published and widely read was John Wise, who advoated democracy, even though he had served a prison term for his radical preaching. Wise's works were circulated throughout the colonies and stirred the people to revolt against many unjust laws. Even though the American Revolution still was some years in the future, Wise actually was the man who did most to start it.

By the beginning of the eighteenth century, the right of trial by jury was established in most of the American colonies. Many of them, including New York, had a system of courts somewhat similar to those in England, with a State Supreme Court set up to decide major cases and appeals.

In the early part of that century, too, many weekly newspapers were started. Benjamin Franklin founded one in Philadelphia in 1728 and in New York, a few years later, a weekly paper was started by a man named John Peter Zenger. Both Franklin and Zenger were early advocates of freedom of the press, a principle that has been a basic part of American liberty ever since.

But freedom of the press was not won without a struggle. In 1735, New York Governor William Crosby removed a Supreme Court Justice who ruled against him in a lawsuit. Zenger criticized this act and the governor promptly charged him with libel.

Two attorneys who sought to represent Zenger were disbarred. It appeared that the case would go to the jury with only the evidence of the prosecution until a brilliant lawyer, Andrew Hamilton, came from Pennsylvania to defend Zenger. His claim was simple: What Zenger had published about the governor was not libel because it was true. Hamilton then produced evidence to prove his point. The jury freed Zenger and ruled that what he had published was not libel.

Ever since then, the truth of statement that is the basis for a libel suit has been a major defense. John Peter Zenger is honored today as an early champion of freedom of the press.

The eighteenth century was a time when England, not only through the king but through Parliament as well, tried to reduce Americans to the class of bondservants or, at best, low-grade citizens who were permitted to exist only as long as they produced profits for England and for British merchants. The Americans were laughed at when they tried to get representation in the British Parliament. Both Parliament and the king took the position that the Americans were inferior and not fit to associate with Englishmen.

The Stamp Act, passed by Parliament in 1765, helped to fan the smoldering embers of the fires started by John Wise a few years earlier. It required that stamps, purchased from British tax collectors, must be affixed to nearly everything, including newspapers.

Many colonial legislatures protested the Stamp Act. In October, 1765, a congress of the colonies met in Boston and condemned the act. One of the chief opponents was Patrick Henry, then a member of the Virginia House of Burgesses.

British officials began harassing American merchants by obtaining general search warrants that permitted them to enter warehouses or board ships to examine merchandise.

James Otis, an American lawyer who had studied British law, took the case to court and argued brilliantly that the general search warrant was illegal; that to be legal, a search warrant must name a specific place to be searched and must also state what the searchers expected to find.

The judge ruled against Otis, but the basic principle never died and it guides any effort today to obtain a search warrant.

As a result of the many complaints by Americans, the Stamp Act was repealed, but, at the same time, Parliament announced it could make any law it pleased regulating the affairs of the colonies and that the Americans had no right to representation.

During the next decade, Parliament made many other laws that the Americans refused to obey. They all amounted to one thing: "taxation without representation." This was one of the major causes of the American Revolution.

The revolt brought together many brilliant and courageous men, whose names are well known to all Americans: George Washington, Thomas Jefferson, Samuel and John Adams, Thomas Paine, Benjamin Franklin, Patrick Henry, James Madison, Alexander Hamilton and numerous others.

Thomas Paine advocated independence from England in a booklet that was widely distributed early in 1776. Patrick Henry also demanded separation from England and shouted to the Continental Congress: "I am not a Virginian, but an American."

Samuel Adams, whose cousin, John Adams, was to become the second President of the United States, spent most of his time urging the people to unite and revolt against England.

Because of the numerous disputes with England that were growing more bitter right along, the first Continental Congress convened at Philadelphia in 1774. There were many arguments for complete independence, but not enough agreed with this viewpoint. In the end, it was decided to send a written complaint to Britain, together with a resolution calling for the boycotting of trade with England.

Parliament ignored the complaint and imposed its own embargo.

War began in March, 1775. In May of that year, the second Continental Congress met in Philadelphia and it continued in session until the fight against Britain had been won. It acted under the Articles of Confederation, most of which was written by Benjamin Franklin. The document was submitted to the colonies for approval, but final ratification did not come until 1781.

By that time, the war was almost over. But the Continental Congress acted anyway, as if the articles were legal. Its first order of business was to appoint George Washington, with the rank of General, as Commander-in-Chief of the colonial armies. Washington was a man of great dignity, sincere and honest, and his authority was never questioned.

Early in 1776, a committee was appointed to draft a Declaration of Independence from Britain. Although the committee consisted of Benjamin Franklin, John Adams, Thomas Jefferson, Robert Livingston and Roger Sherman, the actual job of writing the declaration was given to Jefferson.

The son of wealthy parents, Thomas Jefferson studied law at William and Mary College, was an avid reader and, at an early age, had a great store of knowledge on many subjects, especially government and the law. Despite his wealth, he held democratic views, and the best of his ideas went into the Declaration of Independence.

With only a few minor changes made by Adams and Franklin, the Declaration was adopted by the Continental Congress on July 4, 1776. It was as much a cornerstone of

freedom as the earlier Magna Charta in England and has influenced lawyers and lawmakers ever since. It is urged that
you read it again. It may be found in your encyclopedia, and
an almanac. If you have none of these on hand, you will find
it at your public library.

After the war had ended, the thirteen colonies, calling
themselves sovereign states, were loosely bound together by
the Articles of Confederation. But with thirteen different sets
of laws, many of them conflicting, the organization was not
satisfactory.

Both George Washington and the man who had served as
his wartime aide, Alexander Hamliton, felt that the new nation could not long exist without a strong constitution. Hamilton was the leader in the movement to call a constitutional
convention.

The government of Virginia invited all the states to meet
to discuss a constitution, but only five states sent delegates
to the meeting, which was held at Annapolis, Maryland, in
September, 1786. Among the delegates were George Washington, Alexander Hamilton, Benjamin Franklin and James
Madison, all men of great influence. Their main decision was
that there was need for all the states to send representatives
to a meeting to revise and strengthen the Articles of Confederation.

The delegates returned to their states and during the next
several months, they urged that the larger meeting be called.
Congress, then acting under the Articles of Confederation,
finally called the convention and it assembled in Philadelphia
on May 14, 1787. Delegates from only eleven states were
there at the beginning. New Hampshire sent representatives
later, but none ever appeared from Rhode Island.

Abraham Lincoln, as a young lawyer, and the interior and exterior of the old courthouse at Pekin, Illinois, where he practiced frequently before becoming President of the United States. (Drawn by Harry Fenn from a photograph.)

(LEFT) This figure, which symbolizes "Turning the Wheel of the Law" to the Buddhists, is located at Benares, India. (RIGHT) The upper part of the Code of Hammurabi (about 2100 B.C.), now in the Louvre, Paris, France. The King, Amraphel in the Old Testament, stands before the sun-god Shamash to receive the laws.

Symbolic picture of Moses holding the Tablets of the Laws of God, the Ten Commandments.

(LEFT) Charles the Bold, Duke of Burgundy, dispenses legal decisions personally in 1473. (BELOW) A German law court in session in 1575. The judges wear berets, the lawyers are bareheaded.

(LEFT) *The Trial* is pictured by "Phiz" for *Pickwick Papers,* by Charles Dickens. (BELOW) This humorous sketch of the 1800's is titled *Attorney and Client, Fortitude and Impatience.*

Informality vs. formality in holding court. The old steel engraving above pictures a justice of the peace comfortably holding court in his home, with a dapper young lawyer pleading his case. The drawing below shows the United States District Court Room in the new Post Office Building, in New York City, during the 1870's.

Through law, a country is firmly established in freedom and a world is united for universal justice. (ABOVE) This sculptured panel by Lee Lawrie, in the Nebraska State Capitol, pictures the drafting of the Constitution of the United States. (BELOW) The International Court of Justice in session at The Hague.

The Supreme Court Room in Washington, D. C., and two panels of the sculptured frieze by Adolph A. Weinman. At the top is "Majesty of the Law and Power of Government," with, below it, "Triumph of Justice with Divine Guidance."

George Washington was the unanimous choice for chairman. However, the most active man at the convention and the person who guided it to a successful conclusion was James Madison. From the start it was clear that a revision of the Articles of Confederation wouldn't solve the problems confronting the young nation and it was agreed that a new constitution would be written and offered to the states.

The sessions were not public; any man could speak his mind without having to worry about whether he was pleasing the voters. (Then, as now, politicians often made speeches they hoped would bring them votes.)

There were many angry debates and sometimes the points of view of two different men or groups of men were as far apart as the poles. Madison realized that the only solution was compromise. So did Benjamin Franklin, then eighty-one years old and so feeble he couldn't read his own speeches. But Franklin's views still commanded great respect, even though someone else had to read his comments to the assembly. The great statesman did not want to see an essential part of the structure collapse, even though he might not fully agree with it, so he suggested compromises, which the younger Madison persuaded the convention to accept.

It was easily agreed that the executive, legislative and judicial branches of the government should be separate. It was agreed, too, that Congress should have certain powers: to levy taxes, to control the money system, to regulate commerce, both domestic and foreign.

But the composition of Congress itself posed a problem. Some of the smaller states were afraid they would not have enough representation. The issue was settled when it was agreed that Congress would consist of two legislative bodies

—the Senate and the House of Representatives. Every state would have two senators, regardless of its size. The number of representatives would be according to each state's population.

No law could be passed unless it had the approval of a majority of both the Senate and the House.

There were many proposals for the executive offcer of the government. It was agreed finally that there would be a President (and a Vice President to take over the office if the President died). The President would have a cabinet—a group composed of the men appointed as secretaries of the various government departments, such as the Secretary of State.

The President also would have the power of vetoing any act of Congress. But if Congress felt strongly enough about the measure, there could be a move to override the veto. If two-thirds of the members of both houses voted to override the veto, the measure became law without the approval of the President. (The President's veto of an act of Congress usually stands. There have been very few cases where Congress has voted to override the veto.)

When the Constitution finally was finished and sent to Congress, there was a stipulation that it was to go into effect as soon as it had been approved by two-thirds of the states— in that case, nine. The Constitution itself contained the procedure by which it could be amended. On purpose, the framers of the Constitution made it somewhat difficult to pass an amendment; they considered it to be in the best interest of the nation that there be no amendments without proper thought.

As soon as the Constitution was submitted to the states,

there was a great clamor for amendments, mainly to spell out individual rights. James Madison began drafting these amendments even before the Constitution was ratified.

The ninth state, New Hampshire, approved the Constitution on June 21, 1788, and it went into effect the first Wednesday of March, 1789; by that time, two other states had ratified it. There was never any doubt that the first President would be George Washington. The runner-up was John Adams and he became the first Vice President.

The first Congress to convene under the Constitution sent the ten amendments, widely known as the Bill of Rights, to the states and all ten were quickly approved.

We shall discuss the Constitution in more detail in a later chapter. It established, as Abraham Lincoln was to say later, a government "of the people, by the people, and for the people." Although there are many countries older than the United States, none has had a government that has endured as long. The form of government provided by the Constitution now is the oldest in existence.

Since the Constitution was designed only to cover the broad general principles necessary for the functioning of a free society, each state had its own constitution, based on its own specific needs. The Federal and State Constitutions furnish guidelines for judges, who sometimes are called upon to rule whether or not an act of a state legislature or of Congress is legal.

The Constitution does not give this specific power to the courts. The Constitution provided for a Supreme Court and such other inferior courts as Congress might establish. Since this was rather vague, a judicial system was one of the first things to which the first Congress gave its attention. A committee was appointed to draw up an act.

The result was the Judiciary Act, which established the Supreme Court, with five Justices and a Chief Justice; Federal District Courts and a Circuit Court of Appeals. Federal District Courts had jurisdiction in all federal crimes or actions that came under federal law. The Circuit Court of Appeals would act on appeals from verdicts of the District Courts, and the Supreme Court would be the final court of appeal.

From the beginning, the Supreme Court was called upon to rule whether an act of a legislature of a state or a law made by Congress was constitutional—that is, whether such a law could be made under the provisions of the Constitution.

The Supreme Court also received appeals by persons convicted of crimes who claimed they had not been given fair trials or that their rights had been violated. These are the two basic reasons for appeal today, and ruling on them is the major work of the Supreme Court.

John Marshall was not the first Chief Justice; others served for short terms and resigned. Marshall was appointed Chief Justice in 1801 and served until his death in 1835. Both a businessman and a lawyer, he also had a great mind and was a man of vision. In 1803, he ruled that an act of Congress was unconstitutional and his ruling stood. This established the right of the Supreme Court to decide whether a law was valid.

Marshall established other principles. Even though there were five other justices, Marshall's will usually was the will of the court. He ruled that the federal government's only powers were those expressly stated or strongly implied in the

Constitution; all other powers belonged to the states. He also ruled that the federal government was more powerful than any one state, that in a dispute between the government and a state, the final decision was up to the Supreme Court. These and other decisions by Marshall survived many administrations and many changes in the members on the Supreme Court bench.

Through the years, there were various numbers of justices until 1869, when Congress fixed the total number at nine, which it is at present, almost a hundred years later.

Meanwhile, other men in the government were having their effect on the laws. James Kent was a graduate of Yale, a professor at Columbia University and, from 1814 to 1824, Chancellor of the State of New York. His greatest service was in reviving interest in the English common law. For several years, Americans had been prejudiced against anything British, but they recognized the merits of the English common law. The quality of both lawyers and judges in the United States had improved greatly. Kent's book, *Commentaries on American Law,* became a standard work for lawyers and it led them back to the common law.

When Andrew Jackson was elected President, he proclaimed himself as the champion of the poor man. Many of his energies were directed toward improving the lot of the poor man, and some of the laws passed during his administration were for that purpose.

Jackson succeeded in having the National Bank closed. Banking and finance then passed into the hands of private individuals. Laboring men, whose wages had been paid mostly in goods, now were paid in cash. Public schools were started and it became possible for any child to have a formal education.

For the first time, the existence of women was recognized by the law. They were allowed to own property and had the same property rights as men, although they still were not permitted to vote and still were not classed as citizens.

During this period, the great issue of the day was slavery. There were many acts of Congress and numerous decisions of the Supreme Court, intended to satisfy both sides: the Northern States were opposed to slavery, but the Southern States wanted to keep it. Rebellion by the South was threatened several times.

The Southern States contended that they had the right to secede from the Union, while the Northern States insisted that the South had no such right, that the Constitution bound them all in a perpetual union.

In Illinois, a man named Abraham Lincoln, largely self-educated, became a lawyer and practiced in Springfield for about twenty years, at the same time taking a great interest in public affairs. In 1856, he helped to found the Republican Party.

Lincoln was opposed to slavery, but he did not advocate abolishing it in those states where it was lawful. He ran for the Senate from Illinois in 1858 and carried on a series of debates with the Democratic candidate, Stephen A. Douglas. Although Douglas won the election, Lincoln's speeches, noted for their brilliance, their common sense and their simplicity, were circulated over the country and Lincoln became widely known.

At the Republican convention in 1860, he was nominated for President. He was elected in November. By the time he took up his duties in the nation's capital, relations between the North and South were at the breaking point and the Civil War soon began.

Despite his feelings about slavery, Lincoln made no effort to free the slaves until 1863. Until then, his idea had been that the principal problem was to keep the nation together. But he realized this could not be done as long as slavery existed, so his famous Emancipation Proclamation freed the slaves on January 1, 1863.

Lincoln appreciated that, even with the War Between the States at an end, there would be strong feeling in the North for punishing the South. He made plans for a brief period of reconstruction that would help the South to pick up where it had left off. But before any of his plans could be carried out, he was shot to death by an assassin. He was succeeded by the Vice President, Andrew Johnson. Johnson knew of Abraham Lincoln's plans and tried to carry them out. However, as Lincoln had foreseen, there were many in Congress who wanted to make the South pay for seceding. They passed harsh reconstruction laws that President Johnson vetoed—but these were promptly passed over his veto. As a result, large numbers of men who came to be known as carpetbaggers invaded the South and forced the election to the legislature and to high office many ignorant and illiterate Negroes. The carpetbaggers told the newly elected Negroes what to do. This had an unfortunate result that is still felt in many parts of the South, at least by the older people. Until the War Between the States, there had been an affection between most white people and Negroes. The acts of the carpetbaggers brought hatred.

The Thirteenth Amendment to the Constitution outlawed

slavery in any State or Territory of the United States. This was followed by the Fourteenth Amendment, which defined the rights of citizenship, provided equal protection of the laws for all citizens, and prohibited the states from depriving any citizen of life, liberty or property without due process of law. The Fifteenth Amendment established the right of any citizen to vote regardless of race, color or previous condition of servitude (that is, slavery).

A Civil Rights Act was passed in 1875, but it was held unconstitutional because the court ruled that it tried to enforce social rights rather than legal rights. Other civil rights laws were passed from time to time, but most of them never were strictly enforced. (The most recent was the act of 1964. If you read the daily papers thoughtfully, you know about the struggles that still are going on in this field.)

After the War Between the States, the country expanded rapidly westward, where there still were many frontiers. The six-shooter had been invented and it was the main instrument of the law for many years—almost into the twentieth century. But with the growth of western states and cities, an effort was made to establish proper law and order. By the close of the nineteenth century, most of the West lived under laws similar to those in other states.

The latter decades of the nineteenth century produced territorial and industrial expansion in the United States unequaled in any previous era. A great network of railroads was built from the Atlantic coast to the Pacific coast. Thousands of newspapers, many of them dailies, were established; the telegraph carried news instantly from one section of the country to another and from overseas. Electric light was invented and electric power was produced and harnessed. The gasoline engine was invented and automobiles were put on the market.

Great industrial empires grew, under the control of a handful of men who sneered at the laws and at the men they employed. But labor was slowly being organized and in 1886, the American Federation of Labor was established, with Samuel Gompers as president.

Stirred by the working people who had to labor six days a week, often twelve hours a day, for low wages, writers of the latter part of the nineteenth century and early part of the twentieth century began exposing the powerful industrialists they called robber barons. Many had been ruthless in exploiting labor and many others had bribed public officials to let them do as they pleased.

This brought a reform movement. The first law of great importance was passed in 1890; it was the Sherman Anti-Trust Act, and its purpose was to stop monopolies or combines in restraint of trade. About twenty-five years later, Congress strengthened this with the Clayton Act, which carried a clause urged by Gompers: "The labor of a human being is not a commodity or an article of commerce."

Since then, many great corporations have been forced to give up some of their activities because they stifled competition, restrained trade or were monopolies. For example, there might be several companies manufacturing locomotive engines. If one large company bought all the others and forced all railroads to buy its engines, it would be a violator of the antitrust laws and could be forced, by court action, to surrender some of its business controls.

There have been many attempts at monopoly, but none, except those operated in the public interest and regulated by the government—such as utilities—have been able to survive. Since stifling competition still is tried from time to time by ambitious industrialists, the Justice Department now has a separate department, with a staff of trained lawyers, to take action against any who attempt this.

President Theodore Roosevelt was the first twentieth-century advocate of social and legal reform. He is famous for his credo: "Walk softly, but carry a big stick." The Sherman antitrust laws were used twenty-five times during his administration, but they still did not fully break up the big combines. What they needed was regulation.

Two government agencies, the Federal Trade Commission and the Interstate Commerce Commission, were established, with broad powers to stop unfair trade practices and to determine when a company, such as a utility, could operate a monopoly. The Interstate Commerce Commission was given the power to regulate rates on all public utilities, such as railroads, telephone systems, power and light companies, and the like.

Many state legislatures tackled some of the evils of labor, particularly the long hours women and children were at work. Various laws restricted the number of hours they could work, but it was not until the second decade of the twentieth century that the eight-hour day became common—and nearly two decades after that when the forty-hour work week became the standard.

A man who lived through these developments was a great Justice of the Supreme Court. His father was a physician named Oliver Wendell Holmes, who won enduring fame as a poet. The son, Oliver Wendell Holmes, Jr., was born in Boston in 1841 and became a lawyer. After the War Between the States, in which he served, he became an instructor in law at Harvard. His special interest was common law and his book, *The Common Law,* was widely read. In 1882, he was appointed a Justice of the Massachusetts Supreme Court. He was later elevated to Chief Justice and served until 1899.

He was sixty-one years old when Theodore Roosevelt appointed him a Justice of the United States Supreme Court in 1902. He was a tall man, rather handsome, had a great shock of white hair, a handlebar mustache and a very dignified manner. Those who thought he might retain his position for a few years and retire were disappointed. Oliver Wendell Holmes sat on the Supreme Court for thirty years and did not retire until 1932, when he was ninety.

Quite often, he was in the minority when a case was decided. For example, he felt that too many judges were swayed by their own opinions on social and economic matters, rather than on legal or constitutional grounds. He believed that issues should be decided on the intent of the law.

While he agreed with the purposes of the Sherman and Clayton Acts, he often felt that government lawyers were too zealous in trying to break up some companies which were in the public interest. He warned that the popularity of "trust-busting" might lead some judges to act unwisely. He cautioned that they should always act within the law.

Justice Holmes retired the same year that Franklin D. Roosevelt was elected President of the United States and ushered in a program of social legislation that was known as the New Deal. It came at a time when unemployment was widespread and there was a great economic depression.

Roosevelt initiated so many laws and so much social legislation that there is not space here for a full discussion of them.

Many of the measures he persuaded Congress to pass were challenged as unconstitutional and most were taken to the Supreme Court for ruling. The Court supported most of the New Deal ideas.

During this period, Social Security was established. What it amounts to is an annuity payable at retirement age. To finance it, Congress fixed a tax on wages. The Federal Deposit Insurance Corporation, by an act of Congress, became an agency of the government. Its purpose is to insure bank deposits up to $10,000, so that people will not lose their life's savings if a bank fails. When the period known as the Great Depression began in 1930, hundreds of banks were forced to shut their doors. Because many people feared they would lose their money, they began drawing it out and, as a result, thousands of banks had to close by the end of 1932. To prevent further "runs," President Roosevelt declared a bank holiday in March, 1933. This gave the banks a chance to reorganize. When they were reopened, with bank deposits insured, the "runs" stopped. Since then, very few banks have failed.

Another New Deal measure, the Public Housing Act, permitted people to build homes and borrow money that was insured by the federal government. Banks loaned the money, the loans were insured by the government, and the loans were repaid over a period of years. This stimulated a boom in home building that still is going on all over the nation.

Franklin D. Roosevelt, the only President to be elected for four terms, induced Congress to enact many laws to "make work" for the unemployed. These measures were called pump priming. For young people, there were the Civilian Conservation Corps (CCC), organized along military lines and providing small monthly checks for work that was mostly in the outdoors. Another agency was the Work Projects Administration (WPA), which employed men who were out of work. They did some labor on public works, raked leaves in public parks and swept streets.

By the beginning of World War II, both the CCC and WPA had been eliminated. The President was voted broad wartime powers, and these were not challenged in the courts. Food, clothing and gasoline were rationed; durable goods, such as automobiles and refrigerators, were manufactured only for military use and were not sold to the public. The government put taxes on almost everything as a wartime measure, but many of them are still being collected. Some are or were assessed against goods, such as cosmetics, and others against services, such as telephone and travel.

While the postwar period has been one of great industrial expansion, it has also been a period of great controversy because of the many laws aimed at social reform. Some of these have affected the personal lives of the individual to such an extent that many have charged that the government is trying to control the life of everyone "from the cradle to the grave."

Certain of the laws have led to the charge that there is an effort to stifle individual initiative, that the nation is taking a headlong course on the road to socialism. This trend was slowed down from 1953 to 1961, during the administration of President Dwight D. Eisenhower.

But the tendency toward a welfare state—a close relative of socialism—got a shot in the arm when John F. Kennedy, who called his program the "New Frontier," was elected President in 1960. Lyndon B. Johnson proposed an even broader program of government intervention and was elected

by a landslide in 1964. Mr. Johnson calls his program the
"Great Society," and its many features contain something to
appeal to almost everybody.

How many of his proposals will be enacted into law and
how many will stand the tests of court action are questions
that remain to be answered. There is certain to be a great
deal of opposition from those who believe that a number
of the Johnson proposals will wipe out a great deal of the
individual opportunity and initiative that made America
great. This right to question and challenge is a basic part
of that greatness, too.

No history of American law would be complete without
mention of Roscoe Pound, who was born in Nebraska in 1870.
A man of great intellect, he was graduated from the University of Nebraska when he was seventeen and the following
year, after taking a Master's degree in botany, he entered
Harvard Law School.

He learned a great deal about law, but didn't wait to get
his degree. He returned to Lincoln, Nebraska, where he was
admitted to the bar. He soon distinguished himself as a
practicing lawyer, served as a Commissioner of the Nebraska
Supreme Court and as Dean of the College of Law at the
University of Nebraska.

Pound left that post to become a law professor at North-
western University, moved to the University of Chicago, then
to Harvard Law School, where he had earlier failed to get
a degree. He soon became Dean of the Harvard Law School.
After twenty years in that post, he became visiting professor
of the University of California Law School at Los Angeles,
but he later returned to Harvard, where he occupied the
honored position of Retired Dean.

His five-volume work, *Jurisprudence,* has been called the "Law Book of the Twentieth Century." He has been called America's foremost Architect of the Law.

Among Roscoe Pound's many theories was his belief that law arises out of human experience. He believed that everything was subject to change, but agreed that principles must be recognized, although they are of no value unless they are related to experience.

Roscoe Pound was said to have had such a memory that he never forgot anything he had read—and his reading was voluminous. He lived to the ripe age of ninety-three, and his death was mourned by most men of the law.

# 11. International Law

There was an ancient Greek who was young and healthy, who had a taste for adventure and a desires. They spent many weeks building a boat they lower shore of the Ionian Sea. He found several other healthy young men who had the same desires. They spend many weeks building a boat they hoped would stay afloat in even a stormy sea. They loaded it with food and water and products of their homeland. Then they set a course they trusted would take them to a land across the Mediterranean.

It did. After a long voyage, they landed in Egypt, where they discovered, to their amazement, that there was a city named Alexandria where more than a million people lived. They roamed this new land, trading their products for goods made in Egypt. They found another great city, Cairo, also with a population of over a million.

They learned that the Egyptians had been sailing the Mediterranean for years and carried on a brisk trade at other ports.

Returning to Greece, the young men told of the wonders of the new land they had discovered and sold the goods they had brought back from Egypt. Many of those who listened to their tales were doubtful, but not all.

Soon, many other Greeks had built boats and started sailing the Mediterranean. Trade was brisk and for thousands of years, it was carried on by exchanges of goods. Merchants who had goods to trade usually went along with the cargo and, as a result, on some ships, there might be half a dozen or more merchants.

The jettison rule was one of the first to be developed. If a ship became crippled or struck a rough sea so that some of the cargo had to be thrown overboard to lighten the load and save the ship, the consent of the merchant had to be obtained. Sometimes, if there were several merchants and several shipments aboard, each of them would agree to have part of his cargo thrown overboard or jettisoned.

This gave rise to the practice of insuring cargoes against losses at sea. Bills describing the cargo also came into general use. With the circulation of money among nations, the practice of selling cargoes for cash began.

Numerous disputes arose and had to be settled. Certain rules were adopted by the mariners and, in time, these were generally recognized in all ports where there was commerce by sea. However, many centuries passed before there was any regulation of maritime commerce by conventional laws or by the courts.

If there was a dispute, the merchants set up their own courts and appointed their own judges to hear the cases, which were tried under the rules then in force.

The maritime laws made for Rhodes, the greatest of the

Greek ports, were widely used on commercial ships plying the Mediterranean for ten centuries, even after the Romans had put many ships to sea and had developed a large trade.

In the thirteenth century, the Code of Barcelona, which contained 253 chapters, became the general law for sea traders and continued to apply to Mediterranean shipping until the seventeenth century. It was printed in 1494 and was the most detailed set of maritime laws written up to that time.

With the end of feudalism and the establishment of in-dividual nations, each country began making maritime com-mercial laws of its own. But they were based on the old customs and rules and they were not very different. Mainly, the new laws provided that cases involving disputes and crimes at sea would be tried by the regular courts.

When money came into more general use, the practice of merchants going along with their shipments ceased and a new class of businessman, the broker, did the buying and selling. He would arrange for cargoes to be put aboard a ship, and would get a bill of lading (a bill of loading; lading was an early form of loading) as a receipt. A broker at the port of destination would receive the shipments and sell the goods to others.

The English, who became a sea-faring people, developed their own rules of maritime commerce, but these were not much different from those of other nations. When the first traveler from the West reached China, he discovered that the Chinese, too, had maritime laws that were surprisingly similar to those of the Europeans.

The York-Antwerp Rules of 1890 dealt with insurance losses at sea and were the first general laws applying to shipping. A more complete set of laws was issued at The Hague in 1921.

Other international law, dealing with the relations between nations, or between citizens of different nations, grew largely from custom and practice. There is no international law in the same sense that there is law in a state or country. That is, there is no written law, passed by a legislature and binding on all nations.

Most international law is in the nature of a "gentlemen's agreement." It is a set of rules that have grown from custom and that are honored by most countries. Many have to do with war:

War should be declared formally, by the ruler or the ruling body of a nation. (The sneak attack on Pearl Harbor was a violation of international law by the Japanese.)

Attacks should not be made on churches or on hospitals; whenever possible, civilians should be spared. (This rule was violated freely by Hitler and the other Axis powers during World War II.)

Self-defense is the only real justification for war; the aggressor violates international law.

The use of poison gases and germs is not sanctioned by international law. This rule was violated by the Germans in World War I, but not in World War II.

Ambassadors and the places where they have their headquarters, the embassies, should be protected from attack and the people who work in the embassies, including the ambassador, should be given safe conduct to their homeland.

Prisoners of war should not be killed, but should be imprisoned until they are exchanged for prisoners of war on the other side or released after the signing of a treaty of peace.

There are other international laws that have developed
over the years to govern the relations of nations with each
other in times of peace:

Generally, when a citizen of one country commits a crime
in another country, he is tried under the laws of the nation
where the crime was committed. If a suit is filed by a resident
of one country against a citizen of another, it will be tried
under the laws of the nation where the suit was instituted.
There are some exceptions to both of these rules. For instance, if an alien charged with a crime is an ambassador or
an employee of a foreign government, he may be deported
instead of being tried and imprisoned. Or, if a suit involves
an act or business in a third country, the laws of that country
may apply.

One of the most widely accepted rules of international
law is freedom of the seas. Many wars have been started because the ships of one nation attacked the vessels of another.

Not all nations abide by the rules of international law. The
Communist countries are notable examples. For instance,
many large American firms had business in Cuba by agreement with the Cuban government but, when Fidel Castro
gained power after the Cuban revolution, he soon seized all
the Americans' and other nationals' properties in Cuba and
converted and operated them for his (Cuba's) own use, without any reimbursement to the owners.

Because of the lack of written laws to govern the relations
between different nations and in an effort to establish a lasting peace, the League of Nations was formed at the end of
World War I. It was the dream of President Woodrow Wilson
of the United States. He saw the League as a sort of con-
ference table around which the nations of the world could

meet, discuss their differences and solve their problems like civilized people.

The League held regular meetings for years, but the United States, despite Wilson's urgings, refused to join. It soon became apparent that some nations of the world were not peaceable, that others were set on aggression and conquest, regardless of the League. The League did nothing when Hitler seized power in Germany and it finally folded.

The League did accomplish some worthwhile objectives, however. It set up the Permanent Court of International Justice (now the International Court of Justice), whose purpose was to settle any question of international law, any violation of international obligations, and to fix penalties. There were fifteen judges, each from a different country. During the life of the Court, which turned out not to be permanent, able American jurists served. Our first was John Bassett Moore; the next, Charles Evans Hughes; then Frank B. Kellogg; then Manley O. Hudson; and now Philip C. Jessup.

The Court heard a total of thirty-two cases, in which twenty-four nations were involved. Although there was no law to compel them to recognize its decisions, all nations concerned did abide by its rulings. The Court finally was dissolved for want of legal business. After Adolf Hitler had gained power in Germany, he had violated every known international law, and other nations were doubtful of the Court's ability to cope with the German dictator. Hitler made all the laws in Germany and he violated most of the previously accepted laws of war. Thousands of Germans, millions of Jews, prisoners of war, were murdered by his secret police or in concentration camps, where those who survived suffered unbelievable tortures. He did not resort to poison gas or germ warfare—although nobody knows why he didn't.

When Hitler scorned all law except that made by him, President Roosevelt and others violated many rules of international law. They said it was necessary to defeat Hitler, and maybe this was true, but the result was an almost complete breakdown in international law.

After the death of Roosevelt, President Harry S. Truman gave the order to use atomic bombs to destroy two Japanese cities. This brought a quick end to the war, but it was a violation of the rules of international law—against bombing civilians—and it has been the subject of argument among lawyers ever since.

The victorious Allies created a brand-new rule of international law when they set up a special court at Nuremberg to try twenty-two high-ranking German officials on "war crimes" charges. Special prosecutors and judges representing the United States, Britain, France and Russia conducted the trials.

The indictments contained four detailed counts. Two were for violation of international law, but there were no precedents for the other two. One charged violation of the rules of war, another accused the defendants of crimes against humanity. Both of these were legal charges under the rules of international law.

But the other two, conspiracy to commit a long list of crimes, and crimes against peace, were rules of international law that had been unknown up to that time. Many legal authorities have challenged the validity of these counts, as well as the court that tried them. It appeared to be a case of the victors trying the vanquished. As one authority charged, it was a legal means of wreaking vengeance.

Whether the trials were legal or not, the twenty-two defendants were convicted. Twelve were sentenced to hang, seven were sent to prison and three were acquitted.

Lawyers still discuss the war trials and several books have been written about them. Should you decide to study law, it seems quite likely that you may be called upon to debate their validity.

At the time the war crimes trials were going on, another world organization was being formed. It is the United Nations, now housed in its own buildings in New York City. It got off to a much better start than the League of Nations, perhaps because more nations are members, partly because it has the support of the United States, which the League never had.

All law-abiding people will agree with its purposes—to promote peace throughout the world, to stop aggression by power-mad leaders, to promote harmony among nations, to guarantee equal rights to the peoples of all nations, and to protect human rights.

The Charter of the United Nations is too long to be summarized here. If you have a current almanac, you will find it there in summary with reference to the earlier edition of the almanac in which it appears in full, and it is also available from your public library. It is recommended that you read and study it, then read your daily newspaper to see what is being done.

Whether its dream of world peace and lasting friendship between nations will be realized remains to be seen. But it seems certain that the United Nations will be a strong force in the world for a long time to come.

It has set up many agencies, which are now doing excellent work. One is another International Court of Justice, which has fifteen judges, each elected for nine years; each may be re-elected. It sits at The Hague and hears cases involving disputes between nations. Its record has been good and nations involved have voluntarily abided by its decisions.

It is hoped by many lawyers that the United Nations will evolve a complete set of rules of international law which will be recognized throughout the world; that, in addition to the International Court of Justice, there will be other courts binding on all nations.

One of these, for which I am working, is a World Court of Habeas Corpus, which I consider most important for maintaining the dignity of the individual and protection of human rights.

# 12. World Habeas Corpus

World Habeas Corpus is, at this writing, on the threshold of becoming an accomplished fact, a long-time movement, a tenacious dream that has a good chance of coming true. As we have seen, most enduring laws began as dreams of men of vision, as movements supported by a handful of learned men or as customs. In many cases, decades or even centuries passed before they finally were enacted into law.

Since the World Habeas Corpus Movement began as a result of my efforts, I shall tell you something about it in terms of my own experience, which began before I became a lawyer.

In 1928, in my second year in law school, after a stint with the Chicago Crime Commission, I became secretary and law clerk to Judge Frank Comerford in Chicago. I was captivated by a distinguished Negro lawyer, William G. Anderson, who often appeared before Judge Comerford seeking a writ of habeas corpus. Anderson specialized in such cases and came to be known as "Habeas

Corpus" Anderson. I spent considerable time with him and learned a great deal about the use of habeas corpus as a weapon against injustice.

At that time, two practices were common:

A man would be arrested on suspicion of a crime and, if he did not confess, he would be held without charge. Sometimes, he would be shifted from one police station lockup to another, to prevent his relatives and friends from contacting him. There might be several moves and he might be held indefinitely.

Or a man would be charged with a crime and moved to the county jail, where he might languish in a cell for months, with nothing being done by the authorities to give him a hearing in court or take his case to the grand jury.

The writ of habeas corpus is the remedy for both these injustices. Habeas corpus originally was devised to prevent secret confinement of an accused person. In its present form, an action seeking a writ of habeas corpus can compel the authorities to reveal where the prisoner is held, why he is held, why he has not been charged or why he hasn't had his day in court, and why he should not be released.

After I set up practice as a lawyer in 1930, I indicated to the federal judges that I would be willing to represent persons who were unable to hire lawyers. I received many appointments from Federal Judges James Wilkerson and Charles Woodward and during that year, I used the writ of habeas corpus to win freedom for more than one hundred men.

Later, I learned of forty men who had been held for months in the county jail without legal action. I began proceedings under the old English common law of jailhouse delivery (a form of habeas corpus), which requires a man to have his day in court within thirty days. These men had been in jail so long that the authorities had forgotten what most of them had been jailed for. All forty were freed.

Later, as I was returning from a trip abroad, the idea of a world remedy for people illegally imprisoned occurred to me. Since I was trained in habeas corpus, it was almost inevitable that I would think of it as an international concept.

I began talking about World Habeas Corpus to anyone who would listen. At the time, I hadn't even a remote idea that we would have an international forum such as the United Nations.

A mere handful of men, my former professors—Quincy Wright, Harold D. Lasswell, John Dewey, Judge Floyd Thompson, Dean Shailer Matthews, Dean Roscoe Pound, all distinguished scholars and jurists—and the late George Cardinal Mundelein thought it was a valid and exciting idea. And I received great encouragement from Francis Biddle, who then was Attorney General of the United States.

Most persons regarded me as a young alarmist, certainly not qualified to think and talk in terms of world law. There were many times when I might have given up, except that the devotion of a handful of individuals kept me going. My concept was that the individual is the subject of international law and not the object, which had been the rule for hundreds of years. Being a subject of international law, the individual has the right of remedy to correct a wrong.

When the United Nations Charter was drafted, I tried to get the phrase, World Habeas Corpus, into one of the articles, but Senator Austin cautioned that it might be too disturbing to the Russians and might delay acceptance of the first draft of the Charter.

Nevertheless, the idea continued to grow and the case of William N. Oatis was a perfect opportunity to test it.

Oatis, a native of Indiana, was a reporter for the Associated Press who had been sent to Czechoslovakia, a communist-dominated nation, to report the news. Apparently, something he wrote did not please the communist dictators.

About three o'clock in the morning of April 23, 1951, Czech police went to Oatis' apartment and arrested him. No warrant had been issued and Oatis was not told why he was being arrested. He was denied a lawyer to represent him and his arrest was kept secret. It seemed that he had disappeared and seventy-two hours elapsed before the United States Embassy or his employers, the Associated Press, knew of his arrest.

The United States Embassy, through its counselor, Tyler Thompson, asked permission to see and interview Oatis in prison. But the Foreign Minister of Czechoslovakia denied him this right.

It was revealed later that Oatis was then being deprived of sleep, was being subjected to various forms of torture, and was being "brainwashed" in a ruthless effort to force a "confession."

Eventually, the United States government was furnished with a statement of the charges against the reporter:

1. Activities hostile to the state.

2. Gathering and sending out what was considered secret information.

3. Misusing Czech citizens in order that he could spread false information about Czechoslovakia through illegal news organs.

The charges were not explained or detailed. The hostile activities claimed in the charge were not specified. Nor was there a bill of particulars to clarify the other charges.

Oatis was not permitted to see a lawyer or a representative of the United States up to the time he went to trial, on July 4, 1951. A lawyer with whom he had no chance to talk, a man he had never seen before, was appointed by the court to defend him at the so-called trial. This lawyer, without the consent of Oatis and without asking him, entered a plea of guilty to the charges, which were as vague in court as when they were given to the United States representatives.

It was never explained what specific crimes Oatis was supposed to have committed, or when and where they had occurred.

William N. Oatis was found guilty by the court and was sent to prison in Czechoslovakia. There was every indication that he would stay there indefinitely.

The illegal trial and imprisonment of the reporter caused an international furor, especially in the United States. Congresswoman Edith Nourse Rogers asked for severance of diplomatic relations with Czechoslovakia. Congress passed a resolution declaring that the treatment of Oatis had endangered economic relations with Czechoslovakia.

I wanted to file a petition for a writ of habeas corpus then, but the action was delayed by suggestions that such a move might harm the delicate diplomatic negotiations then going on in an effort to gain the correspondent's release.

But Oatis was still imprisoned in Czechoslovakia after almost a year and there was no evidence that anything was being done to remedy this. It seemed to me that further delays were not justified and I talked to Mrs. Roosevelt, then a member of the American delegation to the United Nations.

She was in deep sympathy with the cause, but she said that the United States delegation could do nothing without instructions from the State Department. I decided to try to find out what the State Department would do if the issue were forced.

On May 8, 1952, through Mrs. Roosevelt, I filed a petition with the United Nations Economic and Social Council, asking action to free Mr. Oatis under a writ of habeas corpus.

That same day, Congresswoman Rogers introduced a copy of the petition in the House of Representatives and it was discussed favorably for more than an hour. Support for the move was building up.

The State Department announced the action, but did not oppose it, as I had rather expected.

On May 16, 1952, the Human Rights Commission reported that the United States would join the action as a "party-movant" (the prosecuting person), and that the petition for the writ of habeas corpus could be filed, with copies of the petition being served on Czechoslovakia.

This exceeded my fondest hopes. The power of the United Nations was about to be tested in the highest realm of the protection of human liberty and dignity.

The writ was drawn up. It is too long and complicated for reproduction here, but I shall list some of the contentions on which it was based:

1. That William N. Oatis is innocent of the crimes charged.

2. That he did not engage in activities hostile to the state nor gather and spread secret information, nor did he spread malicious information about Czechoslovakia through illegal news organs.

3. That he was denied a public trial.

4. That he was unjustly and unlawfully charged, convicted and sentenced for alleged crime which never occurred.

5. That the prosecutors suppressed evidence which clearly established that Oatis was innocent.

6. That his trial was a sham and pretense and actually was a means of depriving him of his liberty without due process of law.

7. That the entire case was a frame-up and a hoax, constructed solely for the purpose of depriving Mr. Oatis of his rightful freedom and liberty.

8. That the conviction of Oatis was secured by the use of false testimony known to be false by the prosecution.

9. That Czechoslovakia, in order to convict Oatis, knowingly, willfully, deliberately and without cause or excuse committed gross fraud in clear violation of the international concept of due process of law.

10. That Czechoslovakia by violating the concept of human rights, which it is pledged and obligated to protect and preserve, violated the international concept of due process principle: "A defendant charged with crime has a right to a fair and impartial trial according to law, and the law does not provide one method for trying innocent persons and another for trying guilty persons, as all persons charged with crime are presumed to be innocent until they are proven guilty beyond a reasonable doubt according to the established methods of procedure."

11. That Czechoslovakia violated another principle of due process known to international law as "the failure to observe that fundamental fairness essential to the very concept of justice."

12. That it is a basic principle that the international con-

ception and requirement of due process, which is the keystone of human rights under the United Nations Charter and the Declaration of Human Rights, cannot be satisfied by mere notice and hearing if a state has contrived a conviction through the pretense of a trial which in truth is but a means of depriving a defendant of liberty through a deliberate deception by the presentation of testimony known to be perjured. That a contrivance by a state to procure the conviction and imprisonment of a defendant is as inconsistent with the demands of justice as is the obtaining of a like result by intimidation.

13. That this case comes squarely within the rules of international law and required all aspects to be tested.

14. That because William N. Oatis was denied due process of law as guaranteed to him by the Charter of the United Nations and the Declaration of Human Rights, his conviction and sentence are void and he should be discharged and set at liberty.

15. That William N. Oatis, having no available remedy to seek effective relief from his unlawful and illegal conviction, has only the remedy of habeas corpus remaining under his rights as a citizen of the United States and as a subject in the world community under the Declaration of Human Rights.

There were other points, but they were technical and need not be reproduced here. The petition was referred to the Human Rights Commission, where it languished for a year. Procedures were entirely too slow. Meanwhile, encouragement came from many quarters throughout the world.

It was proposed that the United Nations adopt the United Nations Writ of Habeas Corpus as a regular legal procedure in a formal petition that was submitted to the State Department.

Various sources asked that the petition be held up thirty days. Within three weeks, William N. Oatis was freed by Czechoslovakia and was allowed to return home. The very threat of action brought results!

World Habeas Corpus may soon be adopted by the United Nations. Moves by the United States government to have it adopted are being generated. However, the idea is embraced by the American Bar Association, the International Bar Association, the Inter-American Bar Association, the World Peace Through Law Center, and many other organizations.

In July, 1964, I presented the idea to more than 1,000 delegates from forty-four nations attending the convention of the International Bar Association in Mexico City, where I represented the American Bar Association. My talk was enthusiastically received and I have had numerous letters from prominent people commending it.

Two organizations of which I am Chairman—Commission for International Due Process of Law, and the World Habeas Corpus Committee of the World Peace Through Law Center —have attracted many eminent men. We have high hopes that world acceptance of World Habeas Corpus, which will establish human rights and human dignity where they do not now exist, will come in time.

Meanwhile, we intend to keep on working to bring this about.

—

# PART III

# PRINCIPLES
# OF
# THE LAW

# 13. Two Sides to Every Case

The motorist blinked in surprise as he suddenly found himself on a wide, dusty street, bumpy, rutted and rough. Facing the sidewalks, made of wooden boards, were several frame buildings of differing heights, none more than two stories high. Some had been painted gray, some brown; others were not painted at all.

Signs in crude block letters were on most of the buildings: Saloon, Livery Stable, General Merchandise, Dry Goods, Hotel, Express Office. In front of the general store were a water trough and a hitching post for horses.

If the motorist had driven on without stopping for a second look, he might have believed he had just passed through a ghost town of the old West. But he didn't go on. He stopped, got out of his car, walked across the porch of the two-story hotel and pushed the door open. Beyond was not a hotel lobby, but open space. He stepped over the threshold for a better view.

From behind, the structures appeared quite dif-

117

ferent. They were no more than bare walls, supported in the
rear by braces designed to hold them up as long as they
were needed. The motorist later learned they formed a stage
setting, a string of props for filming a series of Western
television shows.

More important, he discovered the other side.

Every lawyer knows there are two sides to every case, but
the good lawyer makes it his business to examine both sides.
Sometimes, an attorney makes the mistake of going to trial
with no more facts than those given by his client—the attractive front that is counted on to sway the judge or jury—only
to find out that the supports, the braces that actually hold
the case together, are on the other side.

To avoid such a pitfall, the competent lawyer must learn
all the facts in the case, including those favorable to his
opponent. Gathering facts, most of them rather dull, can be
dry, tedious and tiring work, but it nearly always is rewarding.

Very often, one small fact has decided the outcome of a
dispute in court. For example:

In a midwestern city, a man we'll call Mr. Wilson was
hurrying along a sidewalk on a residential street after a
fairly heavy snowfall. Most of the snow had been shoveled
from the sidewalks and he moved at a brisk pace until he
was almost at the end of the block, where he walked di-
agonally across in front of the small home of Mr. Sims.

The snow had not been cleared from Mr. Sims' sidewalk,
but Mr. Wilson pushed on through it, without slowing down.
He slipped and fell, sustaining minor injuries—a skinned el-
bow and a few small bruises. More angry than hurt, he
blamed Mr. Sims and demanded damages because the sidewalk hadn't been cleared of snow.

Mr. Sims explained that he was not able to shovel snow because he was crippled and quite elderly, but that normally his walk was clean. Today, even before the snow had stopped falling, he had hired a man to do the work. The hired man had been delayed when his car was mired in a snowdrift, but he did come soon afterward to clean off the snow.

This didn't satisfy Mr. Wilson, who filed suit for damages against Mr. Sims. Thereafter, in the legal language, Mr. Wilson was known as the plaintiff and Mr. Sims as the defendant.

Mr. Sims hired a lawyer, Mr. Rogers, to defend him. Attorney Rogers probably would have advised Mr. Sims to settle if the sum demanded had been reasonable, but the lawyer considered the amount far too high for the slight injury. So he set out to learn all the facts.

These were easily obtained from the neighbors, who had been witnesses to the accident. They confirmed that the hired man had arrived in a car shortly after Mr. Wilson had slipped and had cleaned the snow from Mr. Sims' sidewalk. Attorney Rogers also talked to the doctor who had given first aid; he admitted that Mr. Wilson's injuries were slight.

It was apparent now that Mr. Wilson had one of two motives for his suit: His pride had been hurt and he was determined to make Mr. Sims pay. Or he was not too honest and he saw this as a chance to pick up some extra money.

But there was one other possible motive: There could have been a dispute or feud of long duration between Mr. Wilson and Mr. Sims. Very quietly, Attorney Rogers questioned friends and acquaintances of both men. None had ever heard of any sort of grudge held by either man. Convinced that the suit was an attempt by Mr. Wilson to obtain money to which he was not entitled, Attorney Rogers was determined to win for his client. (Every lawyer tries to win, but some work harder than others.)

Attorney Rogers went to his lawbooks and journals, where he found two other facts; now he was ready for trial.

The day came and, as he expected, the lawyer for Mr. Wilson based his claim for damages on a city ordinance that directed every homeowner to keep the sidewalks in front of his property free of snow and ice. (An ordinance is a law passed by the council or governing body of a city or town.)

Attorney Rogers knew the ordinance existed—this was the first fact he had found in his study of the law journals. But when he cited the other fact, the judge directed a verdict in favor of Mr. Sims. This was the other fact:

The same city council that had passed the snow ordinance also had passed another making it an offense to cross a street except at an intersection or designated crosswalk. Mr. Wilson had jaywalked across the street and had approached Mr. Sims' sidewalk illegally.

If Mr. Wilson's lawyer had taken the trouble to learn of the other city ordinance, a "small fact" which was seldom enforced but nevertheless was just as valid as the snow removal ordinance, he probably would have advised his client not to sue. Every lawyer licensed to practice is an officer of the court and it is his duty to discourage any action that he thinks cannot be won, because a hopeless law suit is a needless waste of the court's time and the taxpayers' money.

Even if the jaywalking ordinance had not existed, Attorney Rogers would have been prepared for another course of action because he had taken the trouble to learn both sides of the case. The other course will be discussed in a later chapter.

# 14. The Right to Counsel

The Sixth Amendment to the Constitution of the United States (Article VI of what is commonly known as the "Bill of Rights") clearly states the right of every person to be represented by a lawyer in any case where he has been charged with a crime.

This reads, in part:

"In all criminal prosecutions, the accused shall enjoy the right . . . to have the Assistance of Counsel for his defence."

This means no one may be forced to go to trial without a lawyer to represent him. The accused may elect to go to trial without a lawyer or to act as his own lawyer, but such cases are rare. Usually, the person accused engages a lawyer of his own choosing.

But there are many people, accused of crimes ranging from disorderly conduct to murder, who have no money and no means of paying for the services of an attorney. Since the Constitution provides that the accused shall enjoy the right to counsel, the Court (that is, the judge, who usually is referred to as the Court by lawyers) is obliged to appoint an attorney to represent the defendant.

As a rule, the judge has a list of trial lawyers—attorneys whose work is largely in criminal cases—who are appointed, by turns, to represent persons who have no money to hire their own attorneys.

The court-appointed lawyer has the same duty to his client as if he were being paid his regular fee. Aside from his duty, as an officer of the court, to uphold the constitutional rights of a person charged with a crime, the attorney who works hard for his non-paying client will profit in at least two ways: He will have the satisfaction, the inner reward, of knowing that he has performed a needed community service to the best of his ability; and the zeal of his effort will cause his reputation to spread, bringing him clients who can pay.

In many of the larger cities and counties, there is a public defender whose sole duty is to represent any accused person who cannot hire his own lawyer. He may have a number of assistants, if they are needed and if the county provides the funds. In nearly every case, the public defender works as hard as the prosecutor.

Sometimes, when the public defender has more cases than he can handle properly, the Court will appoint an outside lawyer to defend an accused person without funds. There was an example of this procedure in a large industrial city a few years ago:

After struggling for several years in cramped living quarters, Mr. and Mrs. George Mitchell finally managed to move into a nice, roomy apartment in a tall, new building. There was an extra bedroom for the three children, aged six, seven and eight. The Mitchells had to go in debt to buy the furniture they wanted, but they hoped to pay it off in a couple of years, with Mrs. Mitchell taking a job.

Mr. Mitchell worked in a factory and his hours were from six in the morning to two-thirty in the afternoon. Mrs. Mitchell worked in a hospital as a practical nurse and her hours were from three in the afternoon to eleven in the evening.

Her husband got up early and fixed his own light breakfast. Mrs. Mitchell rose in time to cook breakfast for the youngsters and get them off to school. She had to leave for the hospital before they came home, but, by that time, Mr. Mitchell was there to care for them. He was with them through the afternoon and put them to bed in the early evening. Then, about eleven-fifteen, he would go to the nearby bus stop and meet his wife.

Except on weekends, when both had days off, the two saw little of each other. But they managed and after a year, had paid about half of what they owed. In spite of the hardship, they decided they could stick it out for another year, when the debt would be paid and Mrs. Mitchell could quit her job.

One night, Mr. Mitchell met his wife at the bus as usual and they walked the two blocks back home. Outside the apartment building, they saw some police cars. They went into the lobby, where a crowd of people was gathered. Some policemen were talking to an attractive young woman. Mr. and Mrs. Mitchell recognized her as Miss Linda Morton, who had recently moved into the building. She was sobbing as she talked.

One of the neighbors told Mr. and Mrs. Mitchell that Miss Morton had been in an elevator going up to her apartment when a strange man got in. He pressed the "stop" button, attacked and robbed the young woman, then left the elevator at the next floor, she thought he ran down the stairs.

After the girl had told her story, she was asked to go to the police station to make a statement. As she was walking out of the lobby with the officers, she spotted Mr. Mitchell and stopped. "There he is!" she cried. "That's the man!"

Mr. Mitchell was arrested and Miss Morton signed a complaint against him. He tried to explain that he had been at the bus stop, waiting for his wife, but the tearful young woman insisted Mr. Mitchell was the thief. He was charged with robbery and assault and locked in a cell.

Of course, Mrs. Mitchell knew her husband was innocent; he had been with her at the time the police were called and she knew it would have been impossible for him to commit the crime. Apart from that, she knew that he was a good man and not a criminal.

As soon as she had found a neighbor who would care for the children, Mrs. Mitchell went to the police station. The officers were sympathetic, but they could do nothing. Miss Morton had signed the complaint and Mr. Mitchell had to go to court. The judge ordered him held for the grand jury. His bail was set at $10,000.

Mrs. Mitchell had very little money and nothing that she could pledge for bail. Nor did she have enough to pay a professional bondsman. Mr. Mitchell had to remain in jail until his trial. So many other cases were ahead of his that the date fixed for his trial was two months away.

Having no money to hire a lawyer, Mrs. Mitchell was told to see the Public Defender. But he had so many other cases that he told her frankly he could not offer her any hope for her husband's defense. She appealed to the judge, who appointed a good trial lawyer, James Edwards.

Attorney Edwards found no witnesses who could clear Mr. Mitchell, but he was convinced of the man's innocence. He learned that Mr. Mitchell had never before been arrested; that he had a fine record at the factory where he had worked for ten years; that his pastor and members of his church would testify to his good character.

But Attorney Edwards knew that the testimony of his friends (called character witnesses) would not be enough to win a not guilty verdict for Mr. Mitchell. Almost certainly, the testimony of the victim would be enough to convict him. He believed that Miss Morton honestly thought Mr. Mitchell was the man. It would be almost impossible to make her admit a mistake.

So the lawyer went to the police files. There had been other attacks and robberies in the elevators of other buildings in the neighborhood. Some had occurred while Mr. Mitchell had been in jail. Each victim had described the man and in each case, the description could very well fit Mr. Mitchell.

Attorney Edwards talked to detectives handling robbery cases. They said police were searching for the elevator robber, but he had escaped so far. The hunt for him went on; the detectives promised to notify the defense lawyer if he were arrested.

He was still at large when Mr. Mitchell went to trial. The prosecutor's case was brief. He just had Miss Morton take the witness stand and point out Mr. Mitchell as the elevator robber. She described the crime and was excused. Then the prosecution rested—that is, the prosecuting attorney told the judge that the State had presented all its evidence.

Now, it was the turn for the defense. Attorney Edwards called Mr. Mitchell, who told what he had been doing that evening and flatly denied that he had attacked and robbed Miss Morton. The lawyer could see that the jurors didn't believe him.

Then the character witnesses were called. They told what a fine man Mr. Mitchell was, but this didn't prove he was innocent of the crime. As the court was recessed for the day, there remained only the closing arguments to be made by the prosecutor and the defense attorney.

Lawyer Edwards had a fine speech he hoped would sway the jury, but he never delivered it.

That evening, a detective telephoned to inform him that the elevator robber had been caught and was now in the county jail. The lawyer hurried to the jail, where he was permitted to see the prisoner. He looked so much like Mr. Mitchell that they might have passed for twins!

Lawyer Edwards contacted the prosecutor, who agreed to bring the newly arrested man to court the next morning. (The prosecutor, who is sworn to uphold the law and see that justice is done, has a duty to work just as hard to win freedom for the innocent as to convict the guilty.)

The next morning, the prosecutor and the defense lawyer told the judge of the new turn of events. He agreed to allow Miss Morton to view the other man. She was called again to the witness stand and the real elevator robber was led into the courtroom.

The spectators gasped and so did Miss Morton. She told the judge she had made a horrible mistake. She had falsely accused Mr. Mitchell; the second man really was the robber.

Mr. Mitchell was freed and resumed his life with his

family. The family debt has since been paid off and Mrs. Mitchell now can stay at home instead of working.

But the story might have had an unhappy ending:

Had it not been for the constitutional provision that the accused is entitled to counsel and for the untiring and intelligent efforts of the court-appointed attorney, the case might have ended in a tragic miscarriage of justice.

# 15. The Right to a Fair Trial

The Constitution is the cornerstone of all laws passed by the governing bodies of the United States, ranging from town councils to Congress. Any law that cannot be supported by one of the principles of the Constitution will be set aside by the courts and will cease to have the effect of law.

The most important single purpose of the Constitution is to protect the rights of the individual. One of these rights, which has never been disputed, is the right to a fair trial, which is provided in the Sixth Amendment, part of which reads:

"In all criminal prosecutions, the accused shall enjoy the right to a speedy and public trial, by an impartial jury . . . and to be informed of the nature and cause of the accusation; to be confronted with the witnesses against him; to have compulsory process for obtaining witnesses in his favor. . . ."

Let us suppose that Mrs. Carter was away from home on a shopping trip and when she returned an hour later, she discovered that she had not locked the door. Then she found that a valuable diamond ring was missing and reported the theft to the police.

Mrs. Carter told the police that after she had left, she met Mrs. Seeley going in the direction of the Carter home and had stopped and chatted with her. She saw no one else outdoors at the time. The police talked to the neighbors and found two possible witnesses: one had seen Mrs. Seeley walking toward the Carter home, although she had not actually seen Mrs. Seeley enter it. The other had seen Mrs. Seeley a few feet from the Carter house, walking in the other direction, back toward her own home, two blocks away.

These facts suggested that Mrs. Seeley might have stolen the ring: She had had the opportunity, having passed Mrs. Carter and knowing that she was going shopping and that nobody else was likely to be at home. The door was not locked and she could have walked in the house. Also, it was known to the neighbors that Mrs. Seeley did not own a diamond ring, but she had often said she would like to have one.

Without a law to safeguard her rights, Mrs. Seeley might have been called to account at once. The police might have searched her home and her person on the chance that she had the ring. But the Fourth Amendment to the Constitution expressly forbids that:

"The right of the people to be secure in their persons, houses, papers and effects, against unreasonable searches and seizures, shall not be violated, and no Warrants shall issue, but upon probable cause, supported by Oath or affirmation, and particularly describing the place to be searched, and the persons or things to be seized."

Thus, to search Mrs. Seeley or her home, the police would

have needed a legal paper known as a search warrant. But the facts known to the police created a suspicion rather than a "probable cause," and no judge would issue a warrant on such evidence. If the police had looked through Mrs. Seeley's home, anyway, it would have been an "unreasonable search," which would have been a violation of the rights spelled out in the Fourth Amendment. So the search was not made then.

However, about two weeks later, a persistent insurance investigator noticed that Mrs. Seeley was wearing Mrs. Carter's ring. Now there was "probable cause," and a warrant was issued. Mrs. Seeley was arrested and the ring was held as evidence. This was not an unreasonable search and seizure, because Mrs. Seeley did have the ring. She protested that she had bought the ring and had not stolen it, but she couldn't produce the woman she claimed to have bought it from and she was charged.

As we have seen, she was entitled to a fair trial, but she enjoyed even more protection under the Fifth Amendment, part of which provides: "No person shall be held to answer for a capital, or otherwise infamous crime, unless on a presentment or indictment of a Grand Jury. . . ."

So, before Mrs. Seeley could be forced to go to trial on the charge, the prosecuting attorney had to present what facts he had to a Grand Jury composed of private citizens, none of whom was connected with the court or the police. The facts were related to the jury by the principal witnesses: the neighbors who had seen Mrs. Seeley near the Carter home; the people who had heard her express a desire for a diamond ring; and the policemen who had found the ring in Mrs. Seeley's home.

The Grand Jury voted an indictment, that is, a legal bill

of charges, accusing Mrs. Seeley of grand larceny (that is, a large theft). She appeared in court, the indictment was read to her and her lawyer entered a plea of not guilty. The judge then set a date for the trial and fixed bail. For a fee (usually 10 per cent of the amount of the bail) a professional bondsman provided bail and Mrs. Seeley was released until the date of the trial.

Meanwhile, she had engaged a lawyer who, by working hard, found some witnesses in Mrs. Seeley's favor. The case came to trial and a jury was selected. Under the Constitution, it had to be an impartial jury. Both the prosecuting attorney and the defense lawyer made sure of this by asking each person being considered, among other things: Are you related to Mrs. Carter or Mrs. Seeley? Are you acquainted with either of them? Have you formed an opinion as to the guilt or innocence of Mrs. Seeley?

The twelve jurors seated replied "No" to each of these key questions.

The prosecution witnesses built up a strong case against Mrs. Seeley: Mrs. Carter told of meeting her on the street, of stopping to chat briefly, mentioning that she was going grocery shopping, a chore that would take about an hour.

A neighbor told of seeing Mrs. Seeley walking east toward the Carter home; another told of having heard Mrs. Seeley express a desire for a diamond ring. Then two policemen testified that, on information of insurance investigation, they had entered Mrs. Seeley's home with a warrant and actually had found the ring in her possession. The ring itself was admitted in evidence.

The defense attorney then called his witnesses: Mrs. Seeley admitted having met Mrs. Carter and chatted with her; she admitted passing the Carter home twice. But she said she had not stolen the ring nor entered Mrs. Carter's house—she had visited for about thirty minutes with another woman who lived two blocks to the east. Then she told how she had acquired the ring:

A woman named Flora Collins had come to her door and offered to sell the ring at a bargain, claiming she had to sacrifice it because she needed money quickly. She said she had been referred to Mrs. Seeley by two neighbors. Mrs. Seeley testified she had wanted the ring very much and had enough money saved to pay the price asked by Miss Collins. She bought it because she doubted she would have another chance to get it—or any other ring—at such a bargain.

The next witness was a woman who testified that Mrs. Seeley had visited her for half an hour on the day of the theft. Then two other women were called. Both said they had been approached by Flora Collins, who offered them the ring. Neither needed it and both women referred her to Mrs. Seeley, whose desire for a diamond ring was well known.

The final witness was a detective who testified that Flora Collins was well known to the police as a thief; that a search for her had been made and she couldn't be found; that she was at present a fugitive from justice, having been charged with other thefts.

The jury acquitted Mrs. Seeley.

Thus an innocent person was spared a possible prison term because she had received a fair trial by an impartial jury, as provided by the Sixth Amendment. And the trial itself carried out still another provision of the Fifth Amendment:

"No person shall be . . . deprived of life, liberty, or property, without due process of law. . . ."

# 16. The Right of Privacy

What is the right of privacy? Simply stated, it is your right to mind your own business without meddling by somebody else—as long as you don't poke your nose into anybody else's affairs.

Abraham Lincoln, one of our greatest Presidents, who was also a lawyer and a very wise man, put it in these words:

"I believe each individual is naturally entitled to do as he pleases with himself and the fruits of his labor, so far as it in no wise interferes with any other man's rights."

What are those rights? They are told in simple detail in the Constitution and its amendments.

If you are not familiar with the Constitution, it would be wise for you to read and study it until you understand it, then keep it handy for future reference. In these pages, we shall try to help you to understand some of its basic provisions.

The Constitution is the set of rules that has guided the social and business life of the United States for more than 175 years. It is the best guide to human conduct ever devised by man and it has lasted longer than any set of rules drawn up as the framework of a government. It may be found in your textbooks on Civics or American History or in a good encyclopedia.

Thus, although the right of privacy is broad, you cannot enjoy it without the duties required of you as a citizen. For example:

You may be called upon to serve on a jury in one of the courts in your community. The law requires you to appear if you are summoned. (You may not be selected as a juror, but you are obligated to be in court, ready to serve if you are chosen.) As a juror, you appear in a public courtroom and your name may be printed in the newspapers. So for a short time, you must give up your complete right of privacy.

Or you may be ordered by a court to serve as a Judge of Election. Again, your right of privacy is not complete until after the job has been done, because you will have to meet and deal with the public.

If, by your own choice, you are a candidate for, or are elected to, a public office, you lose most of the rights of privacy, since an elected official is considered to be on duty twenty-four hours a day as long as he stays in public office. Your conduct of the office may be criticized in the papers and on radio and television, but you can't do much about it, since the First Amendment guarantees to the people freedom of the press and of speech.

After you have left public office, you regain most of your rights of privacy, but your actions while you held the office may be talked about and written about as long as they are of public interest.

There are some times when you may lose some of your

rights of privacy through no fault of your own. For example:

Suppose you are in a serious automobile accident or there is a fire that damages your home. This is of interest to the public, and the newspapers have the right to publish accounts of the disaster, using your name. They have this right as long as the occurrence is newsworthy—that is, as long as it is of public interest. When the public interest ceases, you regain the right of privacy.

Perhaps you have wondered why persons who are dead may be criticized by writers or shown in a different light through the radio, television or movies. The answer is that a dead person has no right of privacy; in a legal sense, he ceased to exist when life left his body.

Quite reasonably, you may ask why, if this is so, his will is carried out. There is an answer to that, too: His will was drawn and signed while he still lived. (If it can be shown that the will was drawn after he became sick and was not in his right mind—"not of sound mind" is the usual legal phrase—the will may be canceled by the judge, who must recognize the legal rights of his heirs.)

Another person who loses his right of privacy—and most of his other civil rights—is a convicted criminal. In most cases, he regains his rights after he has served his sentence if it is a year or less. Laws vary, but in most states, a criminal who has been in prison for more than a year loses many of his civil rights (right to vote, travel abroad, etc.) unless they are restored by an order of the Governor. In federal cases, an order by the President is needed to restore all of an ex-convict's rights.

However, if a criminal who has served his time can show

that he has given up his unlawful ways and that any reference to his prison record hurts his chances of getting an honest job, he can take legal action to stop any further reference to him as an ex-convict.

# 17. The Dignity of the Individual

The right to personal dignity is perhaps the most priceless legacy of mankind. Just what is it?

It has been defined in many ways. It is the right to be recognized as an individual member of the human race. It is the right to be let alone, if that is what one wants. It is, as stated in the Declaration of Independence, the right to "life, liberty and the pursuit of happiness."

It is perhaps the only right with which one is born, yet, through the centuries, it has been denied much more often than it has been allowed. Tyrants have trod upon it, trampled it, attacked it with many weapons, issued orders against it, but they have not been able to stifle it.

People have been chained, beaten and tortured. They have been made slaves under brutal masters, but no dent has been made in their pride, their personal dignity, which has shone through the

137

dense fog of pain and cruelty like a brightly lighted oasis in a desert wilderness.

Adolf Hitler tried to subdue many millions of people with his dreams of a master race, but the personal dignity—that is, the human spirit—of his victims survived, although Hitler himself was crushed.

The right of personal dignity—whether it is called pride, the human spirit, the desire to live, to be free and happy or merely the wish to be known as a human being—is a natural right, a God-given right. No man or group of men can kill it.

But some have tried, even in our own country.

Ever since the Constitution was adopted as the basic law of the United States, in March, 1789, there have been many attempts to reduce the freedom it provides. Mainly, these have been attempts to take rights away from the people by granting more power to the government.

Thomas Jefferson, another great President and one of the five men who wrote the Declaration of Independence, fought every effort to take rights from the people and give them to the government.

"That government is best that governs least," he declared.

Yet many others have tried since to take rights from the people and add them to the power of the government. Almost a century after Thomas Jefferson died, another distinguished President, Woodrow Wilson, had this to say:

"Liberty has never come from the government. Liberty has always come from the subjects of it. The history of liberty is a history of limitation of governmental power, not the increase of it."

The right of personal dignity is clearly defined in at least two clauses of the Constitution:

The Fourth Amendment provides: "The right of the people to be secure in their persons . . . shall not be violated. . . ."

And the Thirteenth Amendment gives further meaning to the right of personal dignity: "Neither slavery nor involuntary servitude, except as a punishment for crime whereof the party shall have been duly convicted, shall exist within the United States, or any place subject to their jurisdiction."

The fight to keep the right of personal dignity—and all the other rights enjoyed in our country—has been led by lawyers, a fact of which the legal profession has good reason to be proud.

But the fight isn't over. It will go on and on—and it is probable that lawyers still will be the leaders.

Perhaps you will be one of them.

# 18. The Obligations of a Lawyer

A lawyer may accept anyone as his client or he may refuse to work for anyone who asks to be represented. The decision in the beginning is the lawyer's.

But, if he agrees to take the case and goes on record in court as counsel for any person, he may not refuse to act or to withdraw from the case without the consent of the judge or unless dismissed by client and by order of court. Once he has agreed to work for a client, he is obligated to do his best, without regard to the amount of labor involved.

As an officer of the court, every lawyer—whether prosecutor or defense attorney—is obligated to uphold justice. That is why, in some cases you may have heard about, the prosecutor has asked the judge to dismiss charges against an accused. The prosecutor has learned that the defendant actually is innocent and it would not serve the ends of justice to go ahead with the prosecution.

Or a defense lawyer, after a thorough investigation, may be able to find no witness and no evidence in favor of his client. He may then advise the client to enter a plea of guilty and ask the judge for mercy.

Since the Constitution provides that every person shall have the right to counsel and shall have the right to a fair trial by an impartial jury, the lawyer who has discovered, after gathering all the facts, that his client is guilty, still has a duty to represent him and try to win probation or a lesser sentence.

(When a person is given probation, it means that he is free to go about his everyday business for the duration of the sentence, if his conduct is good and if he does not violate any law. But even a minor violation, such as disorderly conduct, may result in his being sent to prison to serve out his sentence.)

In a civil suit, where one man sues another, damages may be justified, but not in the amount asked. It is the duty of the lawyer for the defendant to try to have the amount reduced by showing that it is too large.

To do this, he will present certain facts in mitigation. This means that he will try to show that the offense was not as serious as it is claimed to be and that the circumstances are less severe.

Let's go back to a case we discussed earlier. Mr. Wilson sued Mr. Sims because the snow was not cleaned from his sidewalk as required by a city ordinance. The judge found in favor of Mr. Sims because Mr. Wilson had violated another ordinance—against crossing a street except at an intersection or properly marked crosswalk. Let us suppose the jaywalking ordinance did not exist. Mr. Rogers, who is serving as lawyer for Mr. Sims, will charge contributory negligence by Mr. Wilson and he will claim mitigating circumstances.

Attorney Rogers will offer certain facts in mitigation:

He will show, by the testimony of witnesses, that Mr. Wilson was walking at a faster than normal pace and that his slipping on the snow-covered sidewalk was partially his own fault. The lawyer will also show, through the testimony of the man hired to clean off the snow, that Mr. Sims had made the arrangements in ample time and that the man hired actually had started out before the storm had stopped; that he had been prevented from doing the job on time through no fault of his own.

Attorney Rogers also will put the physician who treated Mr. Wilson on the witness stand and try to show, by questioning the doctor, that the plaintiff's injuries were not serious.

Finally, through his arguments to the jury, Attorney Rogers will plead that the sum asked is too high and he will request the jurors to limit the damages awarded to Mr. Wilson to what it actually cost him to be treated by the physician.

It is likely that the jury, considering all the circumstances, will award Mr. Wilson a much smaller sum—the cost of his doctor's bill plus a token amount for the injury to his feelings.

# 19. The Rights of a Lawyer

A lawyer may refuse to act when his client asks or demands that he present false testimony. This is covered in an Oath of Admission, recommended by the American Bar Association:

"I will not counsel or maintain any suit or proceeding which shall appear to me to be unjust, nor any defense except such as I believe to be honestly debatable under the law of the land;

"I will employ, for the purpose of maintaining the causes confided to me, such means only as are consistent with truth and honor, and will never seek to mislead the judge or jury by any artifice or false statements of fact or law."

Let us consider again the case of Mrs. Seeley, who was accused of stealing a ring from Mrs. Carter. As we have seen, Mrs. Seeley was able, with the help of her lawyer, to prove that she did not steal the ring, but that she bought it, in good faith, from the woman who did steal it.

But let's suppose that the circumstances were different. Let's suppose that Mrs. Seeley really did steal the ring and that she engages a lawyer to defend her. After the attorney has gathered all the facts, he can find none to support Mrs. Seeley's claim that she is innocent. He concludes that she really did steal the ring.

The lawyer tells her this and suggests a course of action: She will admit that she stole the ring. He will try to show, through witnesses who know of her intense desire to own a ring, that she yielded to a temporary weakness. He will try to show through other witnesses that Mrs. Seeley is not normally a thief and that she has not stolen anything else, to the best of the witnesses' knowledge and belief. He will ask the court for leniency and try to gain probation for her.

But Mrs. Seeley is unwilling to do this. She says she knows how her innocence can be proved. She has two friends who will testify that they were approached by a woman who tried to sell them the ring and that they suggested she try Mrs. Seeley.

"I'll swear I bought the ring from her," Mrs. Seeley concludes.

"But what about this other woman, this thief?" the lawyer asks.

"You don't have to worry about her," Mrs. Seeley replies. "She is in a jam for stealing something else and she's left town. She won't show up in court, you can depend on that."

The lawyer then tells Mrs. Seeley that he will follow the course she outlined, if she wishes, but that he can have no part in offering false testimony to the court and jury.

If she insists on doing it her way, the lawyer then can petition the court to be relieved of the case. Very likely, the judge will permit him to withdraw and Mrs. Seeley will have to try to find some other lawyer who is willing to try to get her off on "false" testimony of which he has no knowledge. Even lawyers can be innocently duped.

Unfortunately, there are a few lawyers who will do anything to win for their clients if they think they can get away with it. But the vast majority of lawyers will take no part in such frauds.

Occasionally, a lawyer is forced to act, even when it is almost impossible. In a large city with many courts, a criminal lawyer found that he was scheduled to defend two different clients in two different courts on the same day.

He asked one judge to postpone the case, but the case had been continued on a few other occasions and the judge refused. The lawyer then asked the second judge to postpone that case and again he was refused.

He couldn't refuse to act in either case, but, naturally, he couldn't be in two places at the same time. He solved his problem by hiring another lawyer, who acted as his associate. Technically, the provisions of the law were satisfied.

PART **IV**

———

ON

BECOMING

A

LAWYER

# 20. Choosing a Career

You probably know men in different professions in your community, whether it is a small city or town or a segment of a big city. The chances are that you are fairly well acquainted with a doctor and a dentist first hand.

Also, you may know of men in other businesses and professions—such as merchants, newspaper reporters and editors, lawyers, accountants, bankers, corporation executives, and men in public service: a Senator, a Congressman, a judge, the head of a government bureau, a mailman, a policeman. The list is almost endless.

Without a doubt, you have given some thought to the career you will choose. It may be, however, that you haven't made any sort of definite decision. If that is the case, then it is urged that you try at every chance to talk to men in the various careers that interest you and find out what they think of the work they are doing and whether they would recommend it as something you should tackle. What they tell you will help you to make up your own mind.

149

Perhaps you have already narrowed the field to a few professions that appeal to you. If that is the case, then your choice should be easier—you will have fewer people to talk to and you can give more time to talking to each of them.

Or perhaps you have almost decided that you want to be a lawyer. Maybe the only thing that keeps you from making a final decision is that you don't know enough about it: how much schooling you will need, the work required after you become a lawyer, the financial rewards and, most important, the satisfaction you will gain from what you have achieved.

This last is by far the most rewarding of all. There is no limit to what goals a lawyer may reach, to what good he may do, to the things he can achieve for the benefit of humanity. History is replete with lawyers of great stature whose works have not been forgotten, such men as Solon, Moses, Socrates, Plato, Cicero, Justinian, Francis Bacon, and the many founding fathers of the United States. Although centuries have passed since they strove for justice, much of their wisdom still guides us today.

Right now and in the future in which you are interested, the man trained in the law will find countless opportunities. If you want to be a state legislator, a Congressman or a Senator—or even if you aspire to be President of the United States someday—there is no better training than the law to serve as a firm foundation for the wide responsibilities.

The law can be a stepping stone to many different careers. Let us consider the case of Erle Stanley Gardner, who is currently the best-selling author in the world.

Before Mr. Gardner sold a story, he was a successful lawyer. But he had a desire to write and, in his spare time, he wrote stories. He had some bitter disappointments, but he kept on trying. In the late 1920's, he became a popular magazine writer. Then, using his legal experience, he wrote his first Perry Mason book. It was an instant success. Since then, there have been numerous Perry Mason stories. If you haven't read any of them you undoubtedly are familiar with the Perry Mason television shows. Even if he hadn't been a lawyer, Mr. Gardner probably would have become a successful writer. But it was with the help of his legal training and experience that he became the popular favorite he is today.

Let's take another example, that of Daniel Dragel. He became a Chicago policeman and an excellent one. He worked his way up to Sergeant, then Lieutenant. But Mr. Dragel was anxious to take a leading part in the fight against crime. While doing good, routine police work, he enrolled for night courses in law. After a great deal of labor and study, he received his degree and was admitted to the bar in Illinois.

But he still was not satisfied. He studied chemistry and obtained another degree. Now, Mr. Dragel is Director of the Chicago Police Crime Laboratory, often said to be second only to that of the Federal Bureau of Investigation in Washington. Through his knowledge of the law, Mr. Dragel has prepared innumerable cases, based on scientific findings in the laboratory, that have stood up in court. His knowledge of the law has made him one of the outstanding scientific detectives in the country.

Wherever your community may be located, you will find that the police are taking an increasing interest in the law. The chances are that one or more of the officers in your police department will have studied law, so that arrest cases can be presented intelligently in court.

Many of the statesmen and other prominent people you

read about in your daily newspaper or see on television news reports started their careers by training in the law.

In an address at Knox College, a few years ago, Robert Szold, a famous New York lawyer, had this to say: "The practice of law still yields opportunity for substantial financial success, as well as for distinguished professional achievement. There is always room at the top."

Mr. Szold expressed many other fine points that are worth quoting and I believe they will interest you:

"By and large, however, the lawyer must look to compensations other than monetary. He may find satisfaction in intellectual activity; in a certain degree of personal independence; in the trust of his fellows; and in the feeling of well-being derived from a reputation for reliability and trustworthiness.

"He also knows that law and order are indispensable to civilization.

"Seldom does the modern lawyer find the stimulus of a great political cause as did . . . Alexander Hamilton in defending freedom of speech. . . .

"Nevertheless, the practice of law may yield satisfaction by way of participation in causes. The lawyer of fifty years ago might have thrown himself into the defense of social welfare legislation, such as the child labor laws. . . . Today, he may find satisfaction in such a public cause as slum clearance, urban redevelopment and adequate housing for the lower-income groups.

"Again, he may feel that the consolidation of power in the great corporations is a social evil, so he may assist the small businessman, or engage in anti-trust work. He may be attracted by such new areas of law as have to do with nuclear energy. He may participate in a Legal Aid Bureau.

"Generally speaking, however, he who has decided to become a lawyer—whether by reason of deductions resulting from the analytical process applied to his situation, or by reason of advice of friends and family, or by reason of instinctive groping (Abraham Lincoln probably had no career consultant)—will find his satisfaction primarily in intellectual activity.

"A lawyer should possess: 1. integrity of character; 2. intellectual curiosity; 3. capacity and desire for sustained disciplined effort; 4. ability to seize upon the essential facts; 5. courage.

"1. Integrity of character involves a scrupulous regard for obligations as a member of the Bar and as a citizen, far beyond the call of duty; a sense of honor; an affirmative unshrinking all pervasive attribute which has no reservations and brooks no qualifications. A lawyer owes loyalty to his client. But he may not forget his obligations to the court. He is an officer of the court (no mere empty phrase) who must temper zeal with integrity.

"2. Intellectual curiosity signifies more than intelligence, however acquired. Information, culture, learning are all good, all essential; more, however, is needed—an inner compulsion to search for the truth.

"3. Capacity and desire for sustained disciplined effort: No one should consider law as a career unless he wants to work. A lawyer practices in an exacting and demanding profession. He must make no mistakes. He must work hard even before he becomes a lawyer. In order to remain at a good law school, he must put in long hours of high concentration. A law school is made, to be sure, by its great professors, but more is it made by its student body. Excellence vies with excellence. Contact of a good student with the functioning minds of his fellows brings out the best in his own.

"4. Ability to grasp the essential facts: An illustrious lawyer, an ex-Secretary of State, in commenting upon the qualities that made a Justice of the Supreme Court one of the greatest in the history of that august body, said that the most severe stricture which one Justice could pass upon another was: 'He did not know his facts.'

"In any legal case the facts are all important. One cannot apply the law unless he knows the facts. A good lawyer, moreover, has the capacity to distinguish between the important and the unimportant, between the essential and the peripheral, between the decisive and the merely interesting. A good lawyer has the ability to wade through a mass of complicated, sometimes conflicting, items, recognize the crucial one and present that one clearly and sweepingly.

"5. Courage: The lawyer must have the courage of his convictions; the courage to defend the client with an unpopular cause; the courage upon which his client may rely; the courage which sets the client's case before and above any personal consequences for himself. . . .

"Lawyers will produce the future advances which will come in this ever-changing world. Not all lawyers will be prominent in the process and achieve fame. Renown is reserved for the few. But every lawyer may share in the work. Every member of the profession should feel that he has a calling, not merely a means of livelihood. He should possess a sense of dedication, which will carry him through the dull periods, enable him to live a full life, and furnish him a vista of personal participation in the work of the world.

"The career of the law affords to the able, diligent student opportunity for a useful and constructive life.

"Please do not choose the law because of default; or because of a vague notion that you may always shift to something else. Do not become a poor lawyer. The national interest in the conservation of human resources should not permit such waste. If you would be a lawyer, be one in the great tradition of the profession."

If you are stirred by Mr. Szold's words—as I think you will be—if you are willing to work hard, then you can make no better choice than the law as a profession.

If you make that choice, there are many things that can help you when you enter law school later:

Regardless of what community you live in, there is a court near you. It may be a circuit court with sessions only a few days a month, presided over by a judge who goes to other communities. Or you may live in a big city, where sessions of court are held every day.

Whatever your situation, it is urged that you attend as many of these court sessions as possible, as a spectator. You will not just hear murder cases, although occasionally you will listen to one of these; you will hear trials of all sorts of legal actions, including suits between individuals and suits against corporations.

You will see at least three lawyers in action simultaneously —the judge, the prosecutor (or the lawyer for the plaintiff, if the case is a civil suit) and the lawyer for the defendant. You will get a very good idea of how the law works, especially in your community, where you may someday be a practicing attorney.

But you shouldn't stop there. Many fine books, both fiction

and nonfiction, have been written about various phases of the law. Space would not permit me to list the books you should read. My suggestion is that you talk to your local librarian, who will be glad to help you find the books that will be of most use to you. These should deal not only with criminal trials, but with all phases of the background of the legal profession, including government, history, police administration and current events.

# 21. Early Training

In high school, long before you have begun the actual study of law, you may prepare yourself in a way that will make your later legal studies much simpler and easier to understand. While you will be required to learn many rules and many principles in law school, you will need to know much more.

Your school probably has several courses in political science, some required, some optional. It is important that you take as many of these courses as you can fit into your schedule—not for just one year, but during all four of your years in high school. Political science deals with government—and you must know a considerable amount about government to be a successful lawyer.

One of the most important branches of political science is civics, which deals with the rights of citizens and the duties of citizenship. As we have seen in the first part of this book, presenting the history of the law, there has been a continuing fight down through the centuries, first for the right to

157

become a citizen, next for the rights a citizen has and finally, what is required of that citizen—that is, his responsibilities— if he is to retain his rights.

If you study this in high school, you will be in a much better position to understand the conflicts that exist today and will arise in the future over the rights of the citizen. Nothing is more important than this, as you may have learned already—and as you certainly will find out soon.

We have seen in the brief outline of the history of the law earlier in these pages that law and the history of a nation are very closely related and, nearly always, one has a great influence on the other. For this reason, it is urgent that you study history, not only of the United States, but of all nations of the world. When you have gained a thorough knowledge of history, you will find it much easier to understand why some laws perished while others have survived for many centuries with only minor alterations.

One of the most important subjects you can take in high school is mathematics. Perhaps only one or two years may be required, but you, the future lawyer, should take every mathematics course you can manage.

Why? The answer is simple: Every mathematics lesson poses a problem of some kind. Through various principles, you will learn to work out the answers to those problems. Some will require reason, others will be worked out through logic.

Every lawyer faces a new problem or many new problems each time he accepts a new client. When you are that lawyer, you will have had your reasoning powers developed and sharpened by your experience with mathematics and you will be grateful that you devoted so much time to that study.

In some high schools, Latin is a required subject, in others
it is optional. If you don't have to take it, you will be
showered with arguments on all sides, urging you to pass it
up. The most frequent will be: Latin is a dead language—
why bother with it?

It isn't that dead. As a matter of fact, Latin is the base of
many languages, especially Italian and the Spanish and
Portuguese tongues, spoken in most of Central and South
America, as well as much of the English language. Even if
this were not true, Latin would still be valuable to you, the
prospective lawyer. For example, *habeas corpus* is a Latin
term, as are many others you will use normally in the practice
of law. Latin was the language of the Romans, and numerous
legal terms and phrases in common use today are directly
descended from the Latin of the Romans. Take, for example,
*res ipsa loquitur, ipso facto,* and *ignorantia legis non excusat.*

So don't let your friends talk you into passing up Latin.
Instead, study as much of it as your schedule will allow.

Most high schools now have student governing bodies, and
participation in such activities will help you later, when you
become a lawyer. You will learn the proper method of dealing with governing officials and you will gain at least an
elementary knowledge of how a government is operated.

You will learn the laws of parliamentary procedure, which
you will have to know in any organization in which you take
part as a lawyer. Also, you will learn to discipline yourself:
when you should speak up and when you shouldn't. As a
lawyer, you will be required to deal exclusively with the
affairs of others; in the student government, your primary
interest will be the welfare of other students.

It is, in addition, an excellent means of broadening your

interests—as they certainly must be expanded after you have become a lawyer and your daily efforts are for others. You will realize very early that you must put aside your own problems for those of other people—your clients.

There are numerous other extracurricular activities in high school and your career as a lawyer will benefit if you share in as many as your time will permit. Participation in a literary society will broaden your knowledge of literature, an asset whose value cannot be evaluated. Most literature deals with the customs of the people; customs were the basis of the laws; and the more you know about the customs of different peoples, the better you will understand their laws—and the roots of those laws that are still with us.

Whether you plan to be a trial lawyer or even hope to be a corporation lawyer who seldom sees the inside of a courtroom, you will gain a great deal if you become a member of your high school's debating team. While a good voice is useful, far more important is your power of reasoning. In a debate, where you must learn to think fast, you will have to call on your reasoning power, and the development of this faculty will be a great asset to you in later years—in the courtroom during a dramatic moment or behind a quiet desk in a corporation law office.

Your debating team also will travel—across town, across the state, possibly even to a distant city. This will acquaint you with other phases of life—and the more you know about life when you begin the practice of law, the more rapid your progress will be.

If it is at all possible, you should engage in your school's athletic programs. These not only will develop you physically, but will instill in you a sense of fair play, a quality that is absolutely indispensable to one who hopes to become a successful lawyer.

Your school—or an organization connected with it—probably sponsors periodic social events, such as dances. Make it a point to try to attend these. A thorough knowledge of the social graces is very important to anyone who comes in frequent contact with other people, as a lawyer inevitably does.

Later, when you have become a lawyer, you will discover that your ability to put a client at ease within a few moments after he has entered your office will help you immeasurably in winning his complete confidence. And that is very important, as we shall see later.

A lawyer is not permitted to advertise, as a businessman does. He must depend for his clients upon the recommendations of others. You can start making friends in high school; many of them may turn to you later when knotty legal problems arise and they discover that personable young person they liked so well in high school has become one of the town's bright new lawyers.

One word of caution: When you engage in these activities, don't go into them coldly calculating how they are going to help you in later years. Take part in each for what it has to offer and what you can give. Throw yourself into it wholeheartedly.

You won't have to worry about what part it will have in your career. Much of it will be stored in your subconscious mind—and it will pop out to help you when you least expect it.

# 22. Prelegal College Training

A prelegal course in college, as such, doesn't exist. Requirements for entering law school vary widely with different law schools. Some require you to have a Bachelor's degree, usually in liberal arts; others require three years of college, some only two. A few law schools will accept you if you have a high school diploma, but there are not many of these.

It is most likely that you will enter a law school that requires a college degree. You may help yourself a great deal by taking subjects that will benefit you later, not only in law school, but afterwards, in your career as a lawyer.

In college, as in high school, you should give as much time as you can arrange to the study of mathematics, history and civics—and for the same reasons why you need them in high school.

But in college, you will have an opportunity to broaden the scope of your learning. Logic is a subject that you should not pass up under any circumstances. Since the days of the ancient

Greeks, logic has been a powerful force in settling disputes, especially in the courtroom. It will serve you well in the years to come.

Sociology is another important subject that is receiving more and more attention in our colleges. It is the science that deals with the origins of people, the relationships between people and especially the relations between an individual and his community. As you can see, a knowledge of this science will prove invaluable to you as a lawyer, because nearly all law arises from disputes between people or between an individual and the governing authority.

An allied subject is psychology; courses are offered in nearly all good colleges. You may ask how that will benefit you in the practice of law. It is a good question and there are some good answers. In the study of psychology, you will learn about the behavior of people and why they act as they do in certain circumstances.

Now, consider this: Many lawsuits—that is, legal actions to get a remedy for a wrong—are settled out of court. Perhaps the number is more than half. Every good lawyer makes an effort to settle a grievance without taking it to court. This knowledge of how people react to certain conditions can be of great value to you in making out-of-court settlements.

Take this example:

Mr. Roberts was behind the wheel of his car, waiting for a traffic light to change, when the rear end of his car was struck by another car, driven by Mr. Hamilton, who had been drinking. Both men got out of their cars and, after an angry exchange of words, Mr. Hamilton looked at the car he had hit and said, "No damage to speak of."

But there had been so much damage that Mr. Roberts had to junk his car. In addition, Mr. Roberts had suffered a minor whiplash injury when the sudden impact had caused his head to snap back and forth. The insurance company representing Mr. Hamilton paid for the damage to the car, but Mr. Roberts wasn't satisfied.

Although he recovered from the injury in about a week, he was put to a great deal of trouble, and the discomfort had caused him to lose about $300 in income. He had to make reports to the police, to the insurance company and the state's safety director. In addition, he had to go to court and tell what had happened to a traffic judge.

He filed suit against Mr. Hamilton, whose lawyer came to see him.

"I probably would have overlooked it," he said, "if Mr. Hamilton had said he was sorry. But he didn't. He was very arrogant and tried to fluff it off as of no importance. That's why I'm suing."

The attorney quickly realized that Mr. Roberts had no desire to make a lot of money from the incident. All he wanted was fair compensation for the suffering the injury had caused him, the cost of medical care and the income he had lost.

After some discussion with Mr. Hamilton's lawyer, who had studied psychology, Mr. Roberts agreed to settle for $500 and withdraw the suit he had filed. This was a good deal for Mr. Hamilton, who might have lost much if the case had gone to a jury, as it probably would have if his lawyer hadn't known something about psychology.

It was recommended in the previous chapter that you study logic in high school. This study should be continued in college, where you will find advanced courses, with more complex problems to solve. When you have become a lawyer, you probably will be amazed at the complexity of some problems and will have reason to be grateful that you learned more about logic.

In college, you will find many of the same activities you were urged to take part in while you were in high school. These will include student government, debating teams and athletics. You should take them again in college, for the same reasons, but you will find that all these endeavors are much more advanced. As in climbing a steep hill, you will discover that the last few steps are the hardest, but your goal, the top, will be your reward.

Other subjects, not likely to be found in high school, should be on your schedule in college. Political science is one of these. You will learn the mechanics of government, how and why men—some great statesmen, others looking for easy money—aspire to public office. In your law practice, contact with public officials of all ranks will be unavoidable. Your cause will be greatly enhanced if you have learned to detect the motive of a public official. He may be a man of the highest principles, he may be a mediocre individual who does no more than is necessary to hold his job, or he may be a man wholly without integrity, one who seeks personal gain while professing to represent the public interest.

Another important subject is economics. The economy of everyday living, of the country itself, is receiving ever-increasing attention by state legislatures and by Congress. Hundreds of laws affecting the nation's economy were not even dreamed of fifty years ago, but they are actualities today and every lawyer must come to grips with some of them. You will do well to prepare yourself in college and to keep abreast of these changing laws and trends in your daily news-paper.

(Here, we may say a word about the frequent references to daily newspapers. If you are one of those individuals who relies mainly on radio and television reports for your news, you are urged to change your habits. At best, radio and television can give you only sketchy accounts, and if you didn't manage to absorb them during their brief coming to life in a newscaster's words or in scenes flashed on a screen, they are likely to be lost to you. A newspaper gives the news in much more detail. If you don't understand or grasp every-thing the first time you read it, you can read it again. A good daily newspaper is indispensable to the well-informed person —and if you're to be a lawyer, you certainly must be well informed.)

If, in the town where your college is located, you have the chance to carry on discussions about the law with a lawyer, by all means, take advantage of the opportunity. If there is a retired judge in the community, he probably will welcome discussions with you. He will like your fresh viewpoints and, almost certainly, he will be delighted to pass on to you the wisdom that can come only from experience.

# 23. Law School

Although law school will give you a good, general knowledge of all forms of law, it would be wise for you to try to decide early in your prelegal training the type of law you want to practice.

Do you want to be a trial lawyer, one who appears often in court, or do you want to specialize in corporation law?

Your decision very likely will influence your selection of the law school you will attend.

Do you plan to set up an office in your home town and accept any clients who come along? Do you plan to be in the field of law what a general practitioner is in that of medicine? Do you expect to be a trial lawyer or to have a general law practice in some city in your state? If so, you probably will want to attend what is known as a local law school.

On the other hand, if you hope to join a corporation law firm or to enter practice with a big firm of lawyers in a large city outside your state, you undoubtedly will go to one of the institutions known as national law schools.

What is the difference between a local law school and a national law school?

Actually, there is not a great deal of difference except in a few factors. Both will give you training in the same basic principles of the law. The national school is likely to be much larger than the local school, although there are exceptions to this.

Generally, a local law school gives more attention to the laws and court procedures of the state in which it is located. The local school also is likely to have professors who teach two or three subjects. They may or may not be authorities in every subject. Even if they're not nationally recognized, the local schools will give you adequate training.

But in the national law school, nearly always a big institution with a large student body, each professor will teach only one subject and probably he will be more prominent and proficient than his local school counterpart.

Also, in the national school, you will give more attention to procedures that will apply in many states, as well as in the federal courts. Usually, a large corporate law firm will not accept a local law school graduate until he has proven himself.

In the local law school, there are fewer students and you will have an opportunity to get acquainted with them, which is good. Each professor has smaller classes, he sees them oftener and he is in a position to give you more individual attention—also good. You will have more opportunity to carry on discussions with your professors and that, too, is to your advantage.

But there are other considerations that you should know before you begin your prelegal studies. Is there a law school close to your home? Do you want to attend that or one farther away?

The cost may be a deciding factor. Are your parents in a position to pay your expenses through college and law school? Can they pay part of the cost? Have you worked during vacations and saved money to help pay your expenses? Do you know of a part-time job you can take to help? Are you in good enough health to work at a part-time job while you pursue your studies?

Previously, it was urged that you get acquainted with a lawyer or judge in your community. Now, it is suggested that you discuss with him the type of law you want to practice and the school you should attend. He will know the lawyers and judges in your city, as well as many of the more prominent attorneys throughout the state. He at least will have heard of many of the country's outstanding lawyers. He will be in a good position to advise you.

But don't hold anything back. Tell him exactly what your situation is: what you would like to do and what you can afford to do; whether your parents will pay all of the expense or whether you must dig up some of it yourself. He will be able to tell you whether any current government program provides loans for law students.

My own experience might be helpful to you. During my years in law school, I worked at several jobs. For a while, I played piano and organ dinner music in a hotel dining room (I had taken piano lessons when I was a boy); I worked as an investigator for the Chicago Crime Commission, my job being to observe court procedure to determine whether the judge was performing as he should; then I was a reporter for the *Chicago Herald and Examiner;* during one particularly lean year, I was a professional wrestler on weekends.

There were other jobs, but these will give you an idea of what it is possible to do. I was determined to be a lawyer. I needed more money than I had, and those diverse part-time jobs provided what I needed to see me through. (I was fortunate in two respects: I had learned to play the piano and organ and my health was good.)

But even though you have sufficient money or are in a position to earn it, you may not be admitted to the law school of your choice. Some schools have more applications than they can accommodate, and they accept only those with the highest qualifications.

At the beginning of your last year in college, make a list of half a dozen law schools you'd like to attend and write to each of them for information about enrolling. You will receive a prompt reply, which will state the scholastic qualifications and the cost. There will be other information pertinent to enrollment.

After you have studied the various factors, make another list of the same schools in the order of your preference. Keep this handy so that you can write to your first choice during the last semester at college.

If, for any reason, you can't be considered for that school, then write to the second of your choice, and so on.

Procedures vary a great deal, but there are basic requirements at all schools: What were your grades in college? Were they very high or did you just squeak by? The larger schools will require a favorable scholastic record and other evidence that you have a good chance of going through law school successfully.

Before accepting you, a law school will want a transcript of your college record (except the last semester, which you will not have finished), at least two letters of recommendation from your college professors, and you must have passed the Law School Admission Test.

The Law School Admission Test is given by the Educational Testing Service, of Princeton, New Jersey. It is required by many law schools and is acceptable to nearly all. You don't have to go to New Jersey to take the test. It is given four times a year at more than a hundred places (usually law schools) throughout the United States.

The fee for the test is $10 and after you have taken it, the results will be sent to any or all of the law schools on your list, if you request this.

However, some schools which require this test will waive it under special circumstances. If you do not have a very good reason for not taking the test, it is suggested that you write to the Educational Testing Service, Princeton, New Jersey, for application blanks. Keep these handy for the time when you'll need them.

When you have met all the qualifications and the law school you choose accepts you, you may want to finish your training as soon as possible. The requirement is three years. How can you do it in less time?

If you begin in June and take summer courses, as well as the regular fall, winter and spring classes, you may finish at the end of the third summer—or a total time of two and a quarter years. You may want to do that if you're anxious to get through school and start practice. On the other hand, you may be depending on what you earn during three months of summer employment to see you through. In that case, you will need to restrict your law studies to the conventional terms.

After you have been accepted, you must decide on your subjects. Many schools have no required subjects, except the twenty required law courses, so your schedule is up to you. But there are basic subjects that every lawyer must know something about. These are the laws relating to crimes, persons and domestic relations, corporations, contracts, real and personal property, torts, agency, negotiable instruments, constitutional law, suretyship, bailments, taxation and insurance, wills, trusts, pleading, conflicts, and others. You will want all these and more, too, if you are going into general practice. You'll need them, even if you are going into a big corporation law firm.

If you have chosen general practice, then you will want to know all you can about torts. We learned something about them in the history of the law. A tort is a wrong against an individual, and the number of these is so great it would be impossible to list them. A tort may also be a crime. A man who is sued by another for a wrong may also be prosecuted for the same act.

In a previous chapter, we related the example of Mr. Hamilton, whose car struck the rear of a car in which sat Mr. Roberts, waiting for a traffic signal to change. That was a tort because it was a wrong against an individual. It was the basis of a law suit.

Let us suppose that Mr. Roberts, instead of suffering a minor injury, was thrown through the windshield and died. In this case, it would be a crime against the public, because

Mr. Hamilton's act had caused the death of another. Mr. Hamilton could be sued for damages by the heirs of Mr. Roberts and he could be prosecuted by the state for a variety of acts: driving too fast for conditions, driving while under the influence of intoxicants, and, most serious of all, reckless homicide.

The lawyer who takes such cases must learn as much as he can, not only about torts, but also about crimes. The actions will be in courts of many kinds. If it's a minor suit, it may be tried in a Municipal Court or even in a court of a Justice of the Peace. It may be tried in a Circuit Court. And, under certain circumstances, it can be taken to Federal Court.

So if you're going to start in and eventually run a general law office, you will need to know a great deal about many subjects. Even though you studied accounting in high school and college, you will want to study more of it in law school. Most law suits concern money, and computation is important in every one of these cases. This is especially true if you happen to take a case involving taxation.

Just how do you go about learning all these things?

Instead of textbooks, you will have casebooks. These are of two kinds: One contains carefully edited, somewhat con-densed accounts of actual cases. The other contains actual transcripts of real cases, which, of course, are much longer.

In class, you will be asked to summarize a case, stating the issue and the decision of the judge or jury. This means taking one of the already condensed cases and boiling it down to essentials. Or you will be asked occasionally to take the complete transcript and boil that down.

Then you will be asked all sorts of questions: Do you think it was a good case? Do you think the lawyers handled it right? Would you have handled it differently? Do you think the verdict of the jury or the judge was correct? If not, what do you think would have been a fair verdict? Why do you think so? What issue or issues were decided in this case?

Everyone in the class will have to study the same cases and, even though you may feel that it won't be your turn on any given day, you should study just as hard as if you knew you would be called on for questioning. There are two good reasons for this:

After you or some other student have been called on for a summary and have been asked questions, the discussion is thrown open to the entire class. Certainly, you can't discuss the case intelligently unless you're familiar with it.

But there is a much more important reason why you should study and try to learn the essentials in each case: Your grade, your mark, in law school does not depend on what you do from day to day in class; it depends entirely on one rather stiff examination you'll have to take at the end of the course. And after you have graduated, you cannot practice law until you have passed your state's bar examination—which is a series of tough examinations on the basic law you have learned.

Unless you can pass the examination in each course, then pass your state's bar examination, you cannot practice law.

This raises some questions that you would do well to answer now, before you have enrolled as a law student or decided on the law as your career: Can you get to the heart of any subject, regardless of the amount of immaterial matter you encounter? Are you capable of reducing a complex set of facts to the essentials? Can you write a summary that is clear, concise and intelligible?

You may not be able to answer those questions now, but here's how you can find out how capable you are:

Take a detailed newspaper account of any occurrence, a magazine article on a fairly complicated subject, or a non-fiction book on any subject. Read whichever you choose carefully, try to determine the essentials and get them fixed in your mind. Then write a summary of what you have read as clearly as you can, keeping what you consider the important points and discarding what you believe to be less important or nonessential.

You'll have to do something like that, not only in law school but also after you have become a lawyer. A client may come to you and give you a concise account of his problem. But it is much more likely that his problem will be buried in a mass of unimportant or irrelevant detail that he'll insist on telling you. To be a successful lawyer, you'll have to be able to extract those all-important points.

So try your hand now. Don't give up after one try or even half a dozen. If, after considerable practice, you find you can ferret out the important elements in a set of facts, then you have an excellent chance of being successful in law school.

All through law school, you should devote as much time as you can spare to the study of cases and issues. They will be very important to you in passing your examinations and later in your practice of law.

# 24. The Bar Examinations

Before you can practice law, regardless of the state in which you obtain your law degree, you must be licensed by the state. To obtain a license, you must pass the examination given by the state's board of bar examiners. In my own state, Illinois, it is known as the Illinois Board of Law Examiners.

But before you can take the bar examination, you must pass a test that is even more rigid. That is, you must satisfy the members of the board that you are of good character, that you will do credit to the legal profession and, most important of all, that you can be trusted with the secrets that your clients will bring to you. In this respect, you are bound by the same principles as those of a minister, a priest or a rabbi. Your client may bare his soul to you, may tell you things he has not told anybody else, and you are obligated not to repeat what he has told you to anybody without his consent.

It already has been pointed out that you, as a lawyer, may go into politics. You may become a prosecutor, a judge, a senator, even President of the United States. In any of these positions, you must be trustworthy. As a prosecutor, you may come into possession of facts that could mean the life or death of an individual; as a judge, you may be required to make a decision that will affect the welfare of many people; as a senator or as President, you may have to deal with secret information upon which would hinge the welfare of the nation—your handling of that information might mean the difference between peace and a war that would cost countless lives.

If, on the other hand, you choose to set up practice in a small town and deal in many kinds of cases, you must have the same basic integrity as if you were a candidate for President of the United States.

Usually, the State Board of Examiners will want your application before you have finished your last year in law school. In some states, the examiners will accept applications earlier. In any case, if you want to lose the least possible time between graduation and starting practice, you should let the board know of your intention of taking the examination at the earliest possible moment.

Rules vary in different states; the information as to when you may apply will be available from your instructors. When the examiners have finished their investigation of your character, they will notify you whether or not you are eligible. We shall assume that your character is good or you wouldn't have chosen to enter a profession where practically everything you do is concerned with helping others.

The state bar examination is the toughest of all the hurdles on the road to becoming a lawyer. The members of the state board, which is always composed of competent lawyers, want to make sure that you are capable of practicing law before they certify you.

You may have learned or even memorized everything you were taught in law school. But that doesn't necessarily mean you are likely to be a competent lawyer.

You will be examined, of course, on how well you have learned the rules. But that is only part of it. Having learned the rules, do you know how to apply them? That is what the examiners want to find out.

Can you take a complex set of facts and use the rules of law that apply to those facts in such a way as to give the best representation to your client? How well can you reason, how independent is your thought? Can you take a set of facts, different from any that you have ever heard before, and work out a good defense for your client, based on your own thinking and logic?

In my home state, Illinois, there are two bar examinations held each year, in March and in September, and both are given in Chicago. You may be examined on any of these subjects:

1. Administrative Law
2. Agency
3. Business Organizations (including corporations)
4. Conflict of Laws
5. Contracts
6. Criminal Law and Procedure
7. Equity Jurisprudence, including Trusts and Mortgages
8. Evidence
9. Federal and State Constitutional Law
10. Federal Jurisdiction and Procedure

11. Federal Taxation
12. State Pleading, Practice and Procedure
13. Legal Ethics
14. Negotiable Instruments
15. Persons and Domestic Relations
16. Personal Property, including Sales and Bailments
17. Real Property (commonly known as Real Estate)
18. Suretyship
19. Torts
20. Wills and Administration of Estates

You won't necessarily have to answer questions on all these subjects, but the board may quiz you on any of them. If, for any good reason, you did not study one or two of the subjects, you may explain why to the examiners and they probably will waive examination on those subjects. For example, suppose you had to pass up one subject because the class in that subject was being held at the same time as another you considered essential.

In recent examinations, four questions were asked on Business Organizations, Contracts, Constitutional Law, Real Property and Torts; three questions on Equity, Evidence, Personal Property and State Practice; two on Agency, Conflicts and Wills, Criminal Law, Federal Taxation, Federal Practice and Negotiable Instruments; one on Administrative Law, Domestic Relations, Ethics and Suretyship.

By the time the bar examination comes around, the aspiring young law student will have gone through study and training that will make all this familiar ground, so don't be apprehensive or worried. If you study with a reasonable

degree of concentration, you will have no problem passing
the bar examination.

"Do not search for hidden meanings, catches or remote exceptions, since none is intended," the examiners advise. "Let
your answer represent your best judgment in each instance
on the plain meaning of the question. In other words, do not
become involved in any intricate game of outguessing the
examiners because they are not trying to outguess you."

Putting it another way, you will be given a problem and
you will be expected to solve it reasonably by applying the
principles of law you have learned.

The examiners have no desire to trap or trick you. Their
sole purpose is to make sure that you are qualified to set up
practice and that you will become a competent lawyer.

As a rule, the bar examiners ask questions on subjects that
seem of most importance at the time. For instance, there have
been many recent court actions throughout the country based
on the Constitution of the United States, so that is a currently
important subject, and the examiners will give more weight
to questions on constitutional law.

There is a time limit for each question, but it is fair and
based on the time you should need to answer. One way to
assure yourself that you will be prepared is to study as many
cases and issues as possible while you're in law school. Take
some of the cases and work out your own solutions before
you read the actual outcomes. In this way, you can actually
begin to practice by rehearsal and be well prepared for anything the examiners may ask you.

Of one thing you can be certain: When you have passed
the state bar examinations, you are qualified to set up shop.

# 25. Learning Trial Tactics

Since juries are composed of human beings, they often are influenced by the tactics of the trial lawyer. I don't mean that the lawyer should be flashy or tricky or a "smart aleck." Too many unorthodox antics are likely to turn the jury against such a lawyer and, of course, against his client.

But a jury often is swayed by the way a defense —or prosecution—is organized, by the smoothness of the procedure, by the sincerity of the witnesses the lawyer introduces. Above all, a jury is impressed by a lawyer who knows his case well.

Many years ago, a well-known lawyer who took me into his office assigned a case to me for trial and he sat in to see how I would handle it. When the prosecutor made his opening address and later when he introduced his witnesses, I was very busy taking notes of points I would challenge or questions I would ask the witnesses on cross-examination.

The lawyer I was working with reached across the counsel table, snatched my notes from me and tore them into small bits. I was puzzled by his action, but I got the message: I was not to make notes while a trial was in progress. Later, he explained:

"You don't have time to make notes while a trial is going on and you really don't need them if you know what is going on. And how are you going to keep up with everything if part of your attention is diverted while you take notes? Even if you take out only a few moments for each note, you can easily miss a very important point.

"The good trial lawyer will file in his memory anything he wants to take up later. If you can't do that, maybe you should not try to be a trial lawyer.

"Every moment of your time at the trial should be devoted to observing. You should watch the jury, the witnesses, even the judge. You should take particular notice of the reactions of the jurors. Your case rests with the jury, so its members are very important to you.

"You should study the reactions of each individual juror and you often will find at least one with certain inclinations that you may turn to your advantage. Quite often, there will be one or more who will, perhaps unintentionally, show sympathy for you or your client.

"How do you expect to find that out if you're busy writing notes?

"After you've found a juror likely to be friendly to your cause, then you emphasize the testimony that you think will appeal to him. Just remember, you need to convince only one juror. He will work on the others. If he can't sway them, at least he will hold out so that the judge will have to declare a mistrial—and that will give you another chance."

That was a long time ago, but the advice is just as good

now as it was then. If you can go through a trial without making notes, you can put the time saved to much better use and will become a better lawyer because:

1. You will have more opportunities to train yourself to remember important points and not clutter your mind with nonessentials.

2. You can study reactions of persons involved in the trial and learn to assess their weaknesses and their strengths.

3. After you have learned to evaluate character through observation and study, you will be able to predict reactions to given situations and use this knowledge to gain favorable verdicts for your clients.

Let me offer you an example from my own experience:

My client was a young man accused of holding up a drugstore. The chief witness against him was the clerk who had been forced to surrender the money. I listened very carefully as he told his story on the witness stand.

He told what I was convinced was a well-rehearsed account. He described my client in minute detail, told other things that had occurred about the time of the stickup, then gave a perfect narrative from beginning to end.

I didn't believe a word of what he was telling except that he had actually been robbed. I was convinced that the robber was someone else, not my client, who was a victim of circumstances. He was a fairly regular customer at the drugstore and he had been there a short time before the robbery. He readily admitted this, but denied any part in the stickup.

After listening to his glib story and watching him closely, I concluded that the drug clerk was not a good observer, that he had not been able to give a good description of the robber. He probably had been careless in the handling of his em-

ployer's funds and was anxious for a conviction. There had
been plenty of time between the arrest and the trial for the
chief witness to memorize my client's appearance and brush
up on all the other things he claimed to have remembered.

My only chance of winning for my client was to discredit
the main witness, the drug clerk. When it came my turn to
cross-examine, I commented:

"Your power of observation is remarkable."

He smirked and nodded.

"And you have an amazing memory."

He smiled smugly.

"You have testified all these events occurred on November
fourth. Is that right?"

"Yes, it is."

I asked him what had happened at various hours of that
day—actually a repetition of what he had told the prosecutor
—and he very promptly gave the same answers.

"By the way," I said, "still speaking of November fourth,
what did you have for breakfast that morning?"

The question caught him completely off guard and he
stammered his reply: "I—I don't remember. Bacon and eggs,
I think."

"Could it have been cereal and toast?"

"I suppose so. I really don't recall."

I had on a wine-colored tie and now I turned away from
him, took a step or two and pulled my coat lapels around my
neck high enough so that they covered my tie.

"What's the color of my tie?" I demanded.

"Black, I think."

"But you're not sure?"

"Yes, it's black."

I dropped the lapels of my coat, faced the witness, then the jury. "As you can see," I said, "it is wine red."

This served to prove that the witness did not have a good memory and that he was not a careful observer as he had claimed in his testimony. The jury soon found my client innocent.

That might not work again. You should be able to think out your own best tactics after a little practice. But until that time, I suggest that you read about different cases and how they were handled. Louis Nizer is one of today's outstanding trial lawyers and he has written some books about his cases. You might find them interesting.

Again, I shall remind you that there is nothing to compare with the real thing, so my advice is to attend as many court sessions as possible, both now and after you have started on your journey to become a lawyer.

Nothing is as effective or as real as watching actual lawyers trying actual cases in real courts.

# 26. You Never Stop Learning

When a diploma is handed to you and you receive your degree in law, your formal education may be at an end, but the process of learning has just started and will continue as long as you practice law. You will learn much, of course, from your own practice, your dealings with your clients, but if you are to be successful, you must learn from other sources.

If you are in a big city such as Chicago, you will want the *Daily Law Bulletin,* which is a newspaper for the legal profession. You will find similar periodicals in other cities; some are published daily, others weekly. In New York, you will find *The New York Law Journal,* in Los Angeles, *The Los Angeles Daily Journal,* in San Francisco, *The Recorder,* and in Miami, *The Miami Review.* In addition to news about important laws, such publications carry legal notices about pending local cases; some, perhaps, might be yours.

The *Journal of the American Bar Association* is sent monthly to all members and it carries many important articles that will help to guide you. You should read them all and keep your copies of the *Journal* for future reference. Indeed, at some later date, you may be called upon to contribute an article on some legal subject which you have handled successfully.

But these up-to-the-minute periodicals still do not give you all you need to keep abreast of the changes that are constant in the legal field. These changes come about in several ways:

1. New laws or amendments to old laws passed by the Congress of the United States.
2. Changes in law or new laws enacted by the legislature of your state.
3. New ordinances or alterations of existing ordinances by the council or other governing body of your city.
4. Decisions of the courts, ranging all the way to the United States Supreme Court, that hold some laws invalid or unconstitutional, or add new strength to other laws.

Obviously, even if you did nothing else, it would be impossible for you to read all the laws enacted by the various legislative bodies and to read transcripts of the proceedings in every court case that affects the law.

However, the larger legal publishing houses do issue regularly digests of important decisions and of important new laws or changes in the old laws.

How much these will affect you will depend upon the type of law you are practicing. For example, every year, there are many changes in the tax laws—local, state and national. Most law schools offer refresher courses in tax law, and if you have difficulty in absorbing printed accounts of the changes,

you will do well to enroll for such courses, which usually are
given at night. The sessions are short enough so that they
will not interfere with your normal law practice.

In addition, the American Bar Association and organizations affiliated with it or sanctioned by it offer seminars at
which prominent lawyers lecture and at which there are
intensive study sessions. The seminars always run for brief
periods—no more than a week and usually for about three
days. They are worthwhile because they can bring you up to
date quickly.

But regardless of how many casebooks, digests or law
journals you read, how many seminars or workshops you
attend, you won't get everything you might out of them
unless you keep up with what is going on around the world.

There are many ways to do this. It is assumed that you
watch television and that you tune in the news. This will
help to give you a broad outline of what is happening. But
you would do well to read at least two newspapers—the
paper that is published in your own city and a reliable one
from a metropolitan center, such as New York, Chicago or
Los Angeles.

In addition, there are several weekly news magazines that
give comprehensive accounts of what the editors consider
important events throughout the world.

A knowledge of current habits and customs has been valuable to lawyers from the beginning of civilization. Remember our old friend, Socrates? Although he made no claim to
being a lawyer, he has long been recognized as one of the
founders of the law. He didn't know much about rules and
regulations, but he knew a lot about people and their behavior. Through his penetrating questions, he learned a great

deal more, which he passed along to his followers. By keeping posted on current events, he was in a position to devise many philosophies, which later were translated into law. Similarly, you may, through your knowledge of people and what they are doing, plus your acquaintance with the law, come up with a novel or unique defense or formulate some kind of principle that will make legal history.

An example is my own plan for World Habeas Corpus. Without a broad knowledge of what was going on in the world, especially in Nazi Germany, where great numbers of people were arbitrarily deprived of the liberty and dignity that is the right of every individual, I doubt that I could have conceived the World Habeas Corpus idea. Although the concept is being accepted throughout the world, it may not be formally adopted by treaty-statute for a long time, but there still is hope—and the fact remains that it has made legal history.

Let's wish that you, by ever widening your scope, may be even more successful.

PART V

—

# THE MANY
# FACETS
# OF THE LAW

# 27. Should You Work Alone?

Almost as soon as you have finished law school, you will be faced with that age-old question: Do you want to be a big frog in a little pond or a little frog in a big pond?

Of course, you have a chance to become a big frog in a big pond, but you can't hope for that status until you have earned it. In the meantime, you have to make up your mind on the other two possibilities, and there are several directions in which you can move. You may:

Set up an office in a small town or city and engage in general practice, taking any kind of case that comes along.

Establish your own office in a big city, accepting whatever is offered and hoping for the best.

Form a partnership to practice in a small town with an older, already established lawyer, whose mantle you will inherit when he retires (provided he is willing to take you in with him).

Form a partnership with another young lawyer,

perhaps one who attended law school with you. You might do this in a small town or a big city.

If properly qualified, go into the office of a large law firm, where you will be employed as an associate on a salary. The partners are the lawyers who own the firm, each having a voice in whatever decisions are to be made. If your work is outstanding, if you display enough initiative and imagination, you probably will be offered a full partnership in the firm eventually. This depends entirely on *you*.

Rent desk space from a large law firm, while maintaining your independence.

Become an assistant prosecutor, in a big city or a small, county-seat town, as a means of starting in politics.

Go into government career service in one of the many agencies that employ lawyers. This is civil service, not politics, although you may later go into politics if you are unusually successful.

These are the principal choices. Let's have a look at them:

If you set up your office in a small city or county-seat town, you will be called upon to handle all sorts of cases, but the work will be on a much more personal basis, because your clients will come from among your friends, the people you meet socially or see around town every day. You will advise a man on many aspects of his life—his insurance when he is first married, the building of his home and buying the land to put it on, any tax problems he may have, making out his will, collecting damages if he or any of his family is involved in an automobile accident. If he dies before you do, you may even administer his estate.

In a small town, you will, as one learned in the law, become a trusted adviser of your clients, but you will generally be called upon as well to voice your opinion on many subjects—whether new lights should be put on the main street, whether the sewage system should be enlarged, and so on. You probably will be asked to serve on the city council, school board and other civic bodies.

You will, indeed, become a big frog in a little pond. Your rewards will not all be in money. Sometimes, your fees will be small and, occasionally, you won't be able to collect at all. But your income should be enough to provide a substantial home and all the comforts that go with it. Above all this is the satisfaction of having served your community and your friends.

However, if this doesn't appeal to you and you want to try to make it on your own in a big city, you have a chance if you go about it in the right way. If you can find a big firm that is willing to rent you "desk space," you will start off with an advantage. Usually, desk space includes the use of a desk, a filing cabinet, a telephone; if you are fortunate, there may even be a vacant room that will be assigned to you.

If the firm is a large one, it will have an adequate law library which will be available to you, and this will be a big asset. If you rent a bare office, you will have to depend on whatever public law library is near you or your local bar association's library. You will be in somewhat the same position as your country cousin, who must depend on whatever lawbooks are available in the office of a colleague, the prosecutor or any county bar association located in the town.

In either case, lawbooks are available from the state bar association and you needn't worry about a shortage of needed reference books—if you have the energy necessary to ask for them.

It is possible to open your own office in a big city, to build your own library while your practice grows. I did that and I'll give you a few hints:

I was unknown and legal ethics prohibited my advertising. I had friends, but not enough of them needed legal advice or the services of a lawyer; many who did already had a lawyer. My initial problem was to make myself known.

First, I went to work (without salary) as an associate of a well-known lawyer, who, as I have related, taught me one basic principle: Never waste time making notes during the progress of a trial, but train yourself to remember everything you need to remember. With him, I served what amounted to a brief apprenticeship, then I opened my own office.

My clients were few and most of those were short of money —this was during the Great Depression. I contacted some federal judges and offered my services in defending people who had no money to hire a lawyer. There were many of these and several cases were assigned to me. My work for each of these was of the same quality as it would have been had I been defending someone paying a high fee. As far as I was concerned, it was my duty to do everything possible for my client.

This paid off for me. The fees I received from the courts were negligible, but I did gain a great deal of experience. I won enough of the cases to attract the attention of the newspapers, who carried accounts of the trials. In turn, my name was seen by prospective clients. They didn't exactly batter my door down, but there were enough of them to keep the proverbial wolf away from that door. Among them were a couple of small corporations—and corporation practice eventually was to become a large part of my law business.

My work had attracted the attention of a political group and at age twenty-six I was invited to become a candidate for Congress. My opposition was a political machine man and he won. I lost that contest, but during the course of the campaign, I became well enough known so that I never had any shortage of clients after that.

If you and another young lawyer decide on a partnership, you may use the same tactics to become known. If you're in a county-seat town, social contacts will be important in bringing you clients who can pay. You may have some who are farmers and have little money, but will make part payment in produce, eggs, and the like. You will make no mistake by representing them, because they need lawyers as badly as others sometimes, and what better recommendation could you have than that of an honest farmer?

If you and another young lawyer form a partnership in the city, you will have an opportunity to specialize in several different types of cases seldom found in the small town—such as income tax, maritime law, labor relations, to name a few. (Yes, people in small towns have to pay income taxes, but very few can afford to hire lawyers for their tax work.)

If none of these appeal to you, then a niche with a big law firm might be the thing for which you're looking. You may be assigned to do research or write briefs or take depositions in civil cases. You may spend most of your time hidden away at an obscure desk, but the work can be very satisfying, especially for one who shuns the limelight of the courtroom. Even though some of your schoolmates may be making headlines with dramatic trial tactics, bear in mind that the work you are doing is important. If it is to your liking, don't worry about making the headlines. In time, if you do good work, you probably will be invited to join the firm as a full partner.

There are many other fields of law you can enter, and we shall discuss some of them.

# 28. Public Service

In addition to the federal courts, which we already have discussed, there are other courts where a court-appointed attorney is needed. The Constitution requires that every person charged with a crime shall be represented by legal counsel.

In the county-seat towns, where all trials for anything above a misdemeanor are held, there might be half a dozen to a dozen lawyers, depending on the size of the town, with perhaps none who specialize in criminal cases. Each of these will be asked by the judge to take his turn at defending someone accused of crime who has no money to employ a lawyer.

Some states provide small fees for court-appointed lawyers; in other states, it is a public service that each lawyer is called upon to render without charge. So, if you decide on practice in a small town, you'll be called upon to do some criminal work in addition to your regular practice.

The situation is different in big cities. In most large cities like, for example, Chicago, New York,

Detroit, Seattle, Portland, Dallas, Washington, New Orleans, Miami, Los Angeles, and San Francisco there are Public Defenders who have a staff of salaried lawyers to handle cases of defendants who are without funds. Most of the men on the Public Defender's staff are young lawyers who need to make a living while gaining experience in the law.

A few lawyers on this staff, those who like the work, will stay on and make it a career. But most remain a year or a few years at most, then move on—some to private practice, others to posts in the office of the State's Attorney, who is the county prosecutor.

With a handful of exceptions, salaries in the offices of the Public Defender and the State's Attorney are not very high, although they are adequate if you can forgo luxury living for a while. The main value of this public service is the opportunity to gain experience in the courtroom and to become known.

For the young lawyer who wants to specialize in criminal law, a term with the Public Defender and another with the Prosecutor is unbeatable training. If you serve on both staffs, you get both sides of criminal law practice—experience that will be invaluable to you when you undertake to defend one of your private clients.

In all the large cities mentioned, the system is very similar although no two setups are identical. To get one of these jobs, you need a sponsor—and, in most cases, your sponsor is a politician. If you are not acquainted with a politician or public figure who has influence, talk to your law professors. The chances are that one of them will be able to introduce you to the right man.

If you stay with the Public Defender or the Prosecutor and

work yourself up to becoming head of a division, you have an excellent opportunity to become Prosecutor or a judge. Your tenure in either office is merely the first step—after you've been a public defender or assistant prosecutor for a few years, you will learn what steps you must take in your own city to advance.

Of course, if you choose public service as a career, there is no limit to the distance you can travel. It's from the ranks of these people that most of our Senators, Governors and Presidents have come.

Just remember the old saying that you, too, may become President someday. You'll need luck and health and a lot of other things going in your favor, but you can help matters along if you want to work hard enough.

# 29. Government Service

The federal government offers many opportunities for the lawyer. Some are political and some are career posts in the civil service.

The Department of Justice is under the Attorney General, who is appointed by the President and is a member of his Cabinet. In virtually every case, the person appointed Attorney General is one who is prominent in politics in his party and usually is nationally known.

Hundreds of lawyers work for the Department of Justice; some are career men and women who stay on year after year, but department heads almost invariably are active in politics. In every city having a United States District Court, there also is a United States Attorney, who is the local representative of the Attorney General.

The United States Attorney has a staff of lawyers, the number depending on the workload—usually governed by the population of the area. Even these lawyers must be sponsored by a political figure to get on the staff.

It is possible to work to higher levels in the office of the United States Attorney, even to become the head man yourself or to move up to the Justice Department in Washington.

The staff of a United States Attorney represent the United States government in court actions, usually in federal courts. They handle civil suits against both individuals and corporations and prosecute any persons or firms who have been indicted for violation of federal laws.

Sometimes, an Assistant United States Attorney will be asked by local slatemakers to run for Circuit Judge. A Circuit Judge who has made an outstanding record very likely will be chosen for appointment to the federal bench. From United States District Judge, several advancements are possible:

If there are several federal judges in your district, one will be selected as Chief Judge. Any of the federal judges may be chosen to fill a vacancy on the Circuit Court of Appeals. Or he may be elevated to the United States Supreme Court, the highest judicial post in the United States and perhaps the most important in the whole world.

The above is a likely line of accession, but it does not always work that way. Any distinguished lawyer may be appointed to any federal judicial post, subject to the approval of the Senate, whether or not he previously had experience as a judge.

An example is Supreme Court Justice Byron White (better known during his college days as Whizzer White because of his prowess on the football field), who was appointed by the late President John F. Kennedy.

If this type of law appeals to you, you should try to make the acquaintance of an influential judge or other political

figure long before you have finished law school. He can help
you to get an appointment when the time comes. He also can
guide you as to what political activity will be required of you
beforehand and after you have the appointment. However,
political influence alone is not enough. It may help but ultimately advancement and recognition depend on capabilities
and character.

If you are not interested in becoming a political appointee,
you still may work in almost any branch of the government.
Every federal agency employs lawyers, and most are selected
from those who have the highest marks on competitive civil
service examinations.

As a rule, when you work for an agency under civil service,
you begin at the bottom level of a scale of salaries prescribed
by an Act of Congress. Periodically, if your work is satisfactory, you will receive a raise. You may merit promotions that
place you in higher levels until you have reached the top.

Perhaps you wonder what a government lawyer does. Consider the Post Office Department, for example:

Postal inspectors receive complaints that an individual or
a company is engaging in fraudulent practices through the
use of the mails. The inspectors investigate and get some
evidence. If the evidence is strong enough, the case will be
turned over to the United States Attorney for further action
in court.

But suppose it is a borderline case. A company advertises
certain merchandise at unbelievably low prices, and all the
orders are handled through the mails. The inspectors receive
complaints, investigate and find that the merchandise is of
very poor quality. It is not what the buyer hopes to get, yet
it probably is worth what he pays for it. Sometimes, it is

difficult or impossible to prove that this is a fraud; the defense is that the buyer gets what he pays for and can't expect to receive high-quality merchandise at such a ridiculously low price. But it is a questionable practice and the inspectors would like to stop it in the public interest. The firm is told that a court action is being considered, but an alternative is to sign a "cease and desist" agreement—that is, if the firm will cease its dubious sales, the court action will be dropped.

The cease and desist agreements always are legal papers and lawyers are needed to draw them up. The Post Office needs lawyers for other things:

For example, a wealthy man dies and three different persons claim his mail. Who will receive it? There may be many factors involved and a lawyer working for the Post Office will have to try to iron out all the disputes that arise and make the final decision. (If the people involved refuse to accept his decision, then the case will go to federal court, where a judge will decide.)

Similarly, all government agencies need lawyers. If such a post interests you, you don't have to know everything about the agency—you can learn that after you start. But if you were going to work for the National Labor Relations Board, for example, it would be very helpful if you were versed in labor laws.

There is a large number of these agencies and if you're interested, you should contact your nearest Civil Service Commission office and inquire about the positions available and when examinations will be given. If you want to work for the government and you show promise, there undoubtedly is a place for you.

# 30. Corporation Law

Probably no other facet of the legal profession offers as many opportunities as the field of corporation law. There are several reasons for this:

New corporations and business organizations are being formed every day; and every day, the business of a large number of existing corporations is being expanded.

There is a continuous flow of new rules and regulations from state and government agencies having influence over business. Many are difficult to interpret and, in most instances, the busy executive does not have the time needed to study and work out the meanings of new government rules. He won't even try; he'll turn the problem over to the firm's lawyers.

A great mass of new law is enacted every year by Congress, by the state legislatures and by city councils. Most of these laws concern business; and there are so many of them—and some are so complex—that lawyers must be employed to determine in what ways they affect the corporation and its activities.

Any firm that does business as usual without reference to new laws is headed for trouble. Nearly all corporations avoid this by employing a staff of lawyers, or by retaining, usually on an annual basis, a law firm that specializes in corporate legal problems.

Although many corporation lawyers make occasional appearances in court in behalf of their clients, many others never go inside a courtroom. Their service is largely advisory. They study new rules made by government agencies, read and analyze the news laws and advise clients as to what they may or may not do legally. If a lawyer's advice is good and if his client follows it, there is rarely any reason for his firm to be represented in a court action.

The corporation lawyer well might be compared with the physician who specializes in preventive medicine. As the doctor tries to prevent disease through advice and medication, the lawyer tries to head off legal trouble by sound advice and solving knotty legal problems.

Earlier, I told you how I came to be a corporation lawyer, after handling a great deal of criminal work. I now have my own office and head my own firm. But you may think that was the hard way to achieve my goal—and perhaps it was.

If you don't want to battle the odds, there is another way to become a corporation lawyer. You offer your services to firms that specialize in corporation law practice until you find an opening. It may be for a seemingly insignificant job, such as working in the law library, doing research, or the like, but it is a step in the right direction and your progress from then on depends largely on how well you apply yourself and the results of your efforts.

In corporation law, as in all other branches, facts are your

most important weapon. Even though you will learn many
facts along the way that do not bear directly on the point at
issue, you will have a feeling for the case and be in a position
to make the essential facts stand out.

Some years ago, I represented a multimillionaire financier
who had been dickering with another financier, also a multimillionaire, who owned a major film studio that my client
wanted to buy. The negotiations went on for many weeks
and numerous legal points had to be clarified, one by one.
The case itself was much too complex to be recounted in
detail here, but I'd like to mention that I, the lawyer for the
financier who was buying the studio, steeped myself in facts
about the motion picture industry. (I didn't *have* to, but I
felt that I must if I were to represent my client with integrity.)

Most of the facts were not relevant to this particular case,
but enough were. When I began assembling the facts I had
gleaned, I didn't know which might be useful. If I had done
a sketchy job and brushed aside a lot of facts because they
didn't seem pertinent, I could not have given my client the
proper representation.

(At the time, I was moderator of a weekly television panel
show originating in Chicago. I had to commute on weekends
between Hollywood, where the negotiations were going on,
and Chicago. This is mentioned to show you that a corporation lawyer does not always recline in an easy chair in his
office—there are many times when he has to burn the candle
at both ends.)

As it turned out, there were several occasions during the
negotiations when some fact that had appeared insignificant
became very important. In the end, we reached an agreement

that was satisfactory to both men. My client was happy with my representation of his interests. Even the other financier, known for his sharp business sense, expressed his approval!

Fully as gratifying as the fee in such a case is the satisfaction of having done a good job. You, too, may experience this kind of fulfillment if you choose to try corporation law, but I hope you won't undertake it unless you are willing to work hard.

# 31. Criminal Law

The practice of criminal law is a specialty that requires a great deal of study and much hard work.
Criminal lawyers are divided into two broad cate-
gories—those who prosecute and those who defend.
Each is essential to our form of government and
to the principles of the Constitution.

Because of certain rules, our system is the best
that has ever been formulated to see that justice
is done, that the guilty are punished and that the
innocent are freed. These dictums are:

1. Every person accused of a crime is entitled to
a fair and impartial trial before a jury of his peers.

2. No person shall be required to be a witness
against himself.

3. The evidence must be presented to impartial
authority—a grand jury or, in a few states, a judge—
and an indictment issued before a person can be
brought to trial.

4. Every person charged with a crime is entitled
to counsel.

5. In a jury trial, the verdict must be unanimous.

6. To find an accused person guilty, a jury must weigh the evidence and each jury must find that the guilt exists "beyond a reasonable doubt."

7. Any person found guilty of a crime has the right of appeal.

There are many other safeguards, but these are the main ones. The rules apply both to the prosecutor and the defendant's counsel. If, during the course of a trial, there is some development that shows the defendant is innocent and has been wrongfully accused, it is the duty of the prosecutor to ask the judge to dismiss the charge or to direct a verdict of not guilty.

The lawyer for the accused can ask the judge at any time to dismiss the case or to direct the jury to return a not guilty verdict. But a judge seldom does this. The exception is when, in the opinion of the judge, the evidence shows the defendant is innocent or that the prosecutor has failed to prove his guilt.

The majority of all lawyers do some work on criminal cases. One reason is that there are not enough lawyers specializing in criminal law. In Chicago, New York, Los Angeles, and San Francisco, for example, there probably are no more than a score of attorneys in these vast cities who work on criminal cases exclusively (excepting, of course, the attorneys in the office of the prosecutor).

Probably the main reason why so few lawyers take criminal cases exclusively is that the majority of people accused of crime do not have the money to hire lawyers. Some handle such cases for small fees or no fees at all, for varying reasons. Sometimes, the lawyer has a strong feeling about the case and wants to free a man he believes is innocent, whether he is paid or not. Others take cases of indigents because their

defense is likely to produce publicity and later bring clients
who can pay good fees.

Before you decide whether to practice criminal law, you
might ask yourself a few questions:

Do you think there is too much injustice in criminal cases?
(There is bound to be some injustice. We can strive for per-
fection, but it is unlikely we'll ever achieve it.)

If you think there is too much injustice, do you believe you
can do something about it? Do you want to?

Do you think that many defendants are not adequately
represented, based on your own observations and what you
have read?

Are you willing to work long hours and run down even
vague leads that might help your client?

Are you ready to seek out reluctant witnesses and use all
your powers of persuasion to induce them to testify?

Do you believe that anybody accused of crime, regardless
of the weight of the evidence against him, is entitled to a
fair trial and to be represented by counsel?

After you have studied these questions and have given
honest answers, then you will know from your own reactions
whether you should specialize in criminal law.

# 32. Tax Law

Since taxes make up the principal income of most governing bodies—the incorporated village or big city, the county, the state, the federal government—the tax laws have become extremely complex. We haven't the space to go into them all here, but we shall mention a few.

To the average individual, a sales tax of 3, 4 or 5 per cent may seem rather simple, and it is to the individual. But the merchant who collects it must not only keep accurate accounts, but he must also report regularly to the state (and, in some cases, to the city, too). Although much of the work is done by accountants, the larger companies employ lawyers to be sure that their reports are accurate and legally correct. (This, too, is like preventive medicine. If an error in this month's report can be corrected before it is sent in, it might result in a great saving in time which would have to be spent if the error were to be found months later.)

Perhaps you think of social security as an insurance or old-age pension. It is both of these, but it also is a tax. With certain exceptions, every employee who works on a salary must pay a social security tax, which is withheld from his pay by his employer.

At the same time, the employer is taxed an equal amount and he must make regular reports and payments to the Internal Revenue Service. Like the sales tax, this is exacting and the employer cannot afford to make mistakes that might be costly to him months or even years later. Most major employers secure the services of both accountants and lawyers to make sure that their social security tax reports are correct.

But the most complicated of all is the income tax. Employers must withhold income tax from every employee, and the amount varies according to the salary and the number of exemptions (there is one exemption for each dependent, including the employee himself). This must be remitted regularly to the Internal Revenue Service and, as with the other taxes mentioned, mistakes can be costly. That is why lawyers are employed.

A lawyer who specializes in tax law may have his own staff of accountants or he may have an arrangement with an accounting firm. He seldom does the actual working of computing himself. His job is to determine that the reports are in proper form.

In addition to the reports on taxes withheld, the firm must file its own income tax, and this often is extremely complex:

When an executive takes a client to lunch, does he do so with the expectation of gaining more business? What if the client's wife is along? Can the full cost of the luncheon be deducted from income tax?

Suppose the client stays in town overnight and the executive takes him to the theater or a night club? Is all or part of of that expense deductible?

Hundreds of such questions arise in connection with the expenses of a corporation, and it is the lawyer trained in tax work who is best suited to answer them. If he submits a report that he believes is correct, he is in a position to answer any questions that may be asked by the Internal Revenue Service, usually much later.

The tax lawyer also will handle the returns of individuals whose income and expenses may be complex. If an individual employs others on a regular salary basis, he must withhold social security and income taxes and make payments to the Internal Revenue Service.

But an individual may have no salaried employees, although others do work for him. He may engage an interior decorator to refurbish his offices, but the decorator is not on a salary subject to income and social security withholding taxes. Everything is done on a contract basis and it is up to the decorator to file his own income tax returns.

Even an individual not on a salary must make periodic payments. If he receives dividends from stocks or bonds, for example, he must file an estimate of his tax for the year at the time that he makes his regular, annual income tax return. This estimate calls for four equal payments, although it can be amended at any time during the year if it appears that the tax originally estimated will be more or less.

The individual who works at a profession has many deductible items that he must be in a position to prove if his tax return is later questioned. For instance:

A doctor's office rent, the cost of light, heat and electric power, obviously are expenses that are part of the cost of doing business. Any ordinary and necessary expense is deductible and the main questions raised by the tax agents have to do with whether the expense was ordinary and necessary. The doctor's lawyer can determine that for him.

Although there are new laws of various kinds every year and minor changes in many laws periodically, there are major changes in the tax laws almost every year. Even if the actual changes in the law may be minor, the Internal Revenue Service constantly issues new regulations so that there really are major changes every year.

In the Internal Revenue itself, there are lawyers who work for the government. Sometimes, a young lawyer works for the Internal Revenue Service to gain experience, then sets up private practice in tax law.

That may be a good way for you to proceed, if you're interested in this type of practice.

# 33. Expanding International Law

There is no body of law, no set of rules to govern the whole world. In the sense that the United States has written statutes passed by Congress to govern certain phases of our lives, there is no international law.

Until very recently, most international law was a matter of custom, of understandings between nations based on these customs. The only written laws were those contained in treaties and agreements.

In the past fifty years and especially since World War II, there have been many treaties and agreements that have the full force of law and actually constitute what we know as international law. The United Nations has been a moving force in these developments and has become a sort of clearing house for agreements between nations.

There are many organizations, now allied with the United Nations, having rules to which many

217

nations have subscribed. For example, there is the Universal Postal Union, which affects the everyday lives of nearly everybody.

If you want to mail a letter to a friend in England, you put a specified amount in stamps on the letter, drop it in a mail-box and forget about it. Or if you want it to go faster, you put on more postage for each half ounce and mail it. In either case, the letter will be delivered, just as it would be if it were addressed to someone in the next county. Similarly, your friend or a business firm in England can send a letter to you and it will be delivered promptly.

Of course, this didn't just happen. It is the result of an agreement on rates and rules of transit and delivery, worked out by the Universal Postal Union, which has laws governing transportation and delivery of all classes of mail, under what circumstances the sender may be paid for any loss incurred in the mails, and what may not be sent by mail, to name a few.

The Pan-American Postal Union is a similar organization whose laws govern mail between countries of the Western Hemisphere.

Not so many years ago, telephone communication between the United States and a country overseas did not exist. Now, you may pick up your receiver, give a number in any of numerous foreign countries and be connected quickly with your party at the other end.

This didn't just happen, either. The fairly smooth system we have now was worked out by the International Tele-communications Union, also affiliated with the United Nations. A major hurdle, of course, was overcoming technical problems, but there were many legal problems, too: crossing boundaries of various countries and fixing rates to which all countries could agree.

The countries who signed the United Nations Charter actually executed a legal document, as binding as a treaty, which brought more phases of international law to those countries than they had ever known in all recorded history combined.

The lawyer may think he will confine his efforts to domestic matters and steer clear of international law, but he is likely to find that he is involved in foreign litigation that can't be avoided if he is to retain his client.

The several organizations that have come into existence through the influence of the United Nations have changed international law from a multitude of unwritten rules to actual, written agreements to which various nations have bound themselves through the signatures of their officials.

For another example, the International Civil Aviation Organization came into existence to regulate air traffic between nations. Without agreements between nations, a jet loaded with 150 civilian passengers might be shot down the moment it crossed a certain foreign border. Of course, nothing like that happens where, through the International Civil Aviation Organization, there is an agreement for jets of both nations involved to land on each other's soil. The jet is scheduled, its appearance is expected and the arrival in the foreign country is routine, except in Soviet Russia and Red China.

However, many problems may arise—how safe a plane must be to be permitted to land, the number of pounds it is allowed to carry, when it can carry mail or other cargo, etc. The International Civil Aviation Organization has rules to answer all these questions.

Many financiers, especially in the United States, want to

invest money in foreign securities or in foreign enterprise. There are agreements covering these projects with many nations now and it is the duty of the lawyer to look these up so that he can advise the financiers which propositions appear to be the safest.

International law is still in the process of development—through the United Nations, and through agreements nurtured by the numerous groups allied with the UN, such as the World Health Organization, the International Bank for Reconstruction and Development, the International Labor Organization, the International Trade Organization, and many others.

In law school, you will have the opportunity to learn more about the United Nations and the bodies affiliated with it. In the library, you will find many publications dealing with the work of the United Nations and the other allied organizations.

Whether or not you plan to specialize in this growing field, you will do well to observe developments in international agreements and the progress of various world organizations. The jet plane and space travel have shrunk the world so much that what was days away may be just around the corner by the time you finish law school!

# 34. Other Specialties

There are almost innumerable fields that offer opportunities for the young lawyer. Even if you choose to go into general practice, you will need to specialize in at least a few of them.

The legal work connected with estates and setting up trusts could occupy your full time if you live in a city where there are many wealthy people. You might, in time, have a practice of your own in this field, but to begin, you will do well to become connected with a bank or other financial institution.

Scores of large banks now maintain trust departments whose only business is working with people who want to stipulate while they are still alive what will happen to their estates—cash, securities and property of all kinds—after they are dead.

An extremely wealthy man may have his own private lawyer, but the majority of people setting up trusts work through ranks. Of course, lawyers do the actual work; usually, they are full-time employees of banks. In smaller cities and towns, the work may be delegated to a trust officer, who will call on a local lawyer—you, perhaps, if you are in general practice in that area and if you are acquainted with the working of a trust.

The client who goes to the trust office of a bank may ask you to draw up his will, in addition to setting up a trust.

You may ask why a man sets up a trust to begin with. This is the usual answer:

A wealthy man wants to leave equal shares of his estate to his wife and two children. He knows that his wife is easily influenced and he is afraid that, if she has a large amount of money at her disposal, she may be induced by some smooth-talking fellow to make an "investment" that actually is a swindle. Her husband wants her to be safely provided for, so he puts the money in trust, to be invested in bonds or reliable securities that will give her a good income as long as she lives.

The children, a son and daughter, may be considered extravagant by the father, who, consequently, puts the money they will inherit in trust until each reaches what he considers a mature age—thirty, thirty-five or even forty. Until that time, each receives the income from the money put in trust. At the specified age, the son and daughter receive the full amount, to do with as they please.

This, of course, is a simple explanation of one kind of trust. There are all sorts, with many varying provisions. For example, a widow whose income is $10,000 a year from a trust may have a serious illness, a long stay in the hospital or some other catastrophe. Usually, there is a provision that the trust may be "invaded" by the executors and some of the principal given to the widow to cover these unusual expenses.

The executors or administrators of a trust usually are officers of the bank, including lawyers. Much of the handling of a trust is left to their discretion. The work of a lawyer on a trust may be of inestimable value.

Sometimes, when a very wealthy man with widespread holdings and business interests makes his will, he sets up an estate to carry on the business enterprises after he has died—until such time as the administrators consider it advantageous to liquidate. Usually, the heirs of an estate that remains active for a number of years share in the income and eventually in the principal.

Invariably, lawyers are needed not only to draw up the papers originally, but to continue to advise while the estate is being administered and liquidated.

Since World War II, there has been a tremendous upsurge in home building and, consequently, in the sale of real estate. A man may buy a vacant lot and build a house without the advice of a lawyer, but one who does this runs the risk of much trouble later. The lawyer will check the title and make sure that it is clear. He will assemble an official history of that particular property in a document known as an abstract. It may date back to a time when the property was turned over to the government by an Indian tribe as the result of a treaty. Ownership from that time on will be recorded in the abstract.

Let us suppose that the tract in question was originally part of a large estate. A family took up residence on the land years ago without buying it. The land was not actively used by the real owner, but, after a lapse of time, he had an opportunity to sell his big tract to a company planning a subdivision.

Meanwhile, the family or the descendants of the family who illegally occupied a small lot on the tract decide to sell it. The buyer doesn't bother with a lawyer or an abstract. He just gets a deed and moves in. Then, perhaps a year later, work begins on the subdivision of the entire tract. Surveyors, who have an abstract, discover that a lot in the tract is occupied by a man who believes the property is his, who has paid another man for it, and who holds a deed that he thinks is valid—but it is not.

When the development firm discovers the error, a number of actions may result:

1. The company, recognizing that it faces a legal fight that could be more costly than the land, issues a legal deed to the man claiming ownership and the case is closed.

2. The purchaser, realizing that he has been duped, may surrender the land and try to recover his money through a lawsuit.

3. If neither party to the dispute will yield, the developer will take the case to court. Whether or not the occupant is evicted as a result of this action, his court costs will be more than he would have had to pay if he had engaged a lawyer in the first place.

In any of these instances, lawyers will be involved.

Indeed, lawyers are required in a multitude of human endeavors. Here are a few:

Domestic relations in which family disputes over ownership of property, over custody of a child, over conduct in the home, are taken to court.

Suits for damages: A man has hit your car while you're in it. You sue for repairs to the car and for any personal damage.

Your pet dog is struck by another's automobile. You sue

for the injuries and the special damages of actual medical bills.

A missing bicycle of standard manufacture is claimed by another to belong to him. You sue to establish title by producing your purchase papers and the registration number of the bicycle and, if possible, bring in the person who sold the bicycle.

A girl's best suit is ruined by splashing paint as she walks alongside a building. She may sue the owner who ordered the painting done and also the painter for actual damages in replacing the ruined suit or just for the amount of her cleaning bill. There is no recovery here for anguish or embarrassment.

Suit for separate maintenance: A husband and wife have separated and the wife goes to court to ask the judge to compel the husband to give her a reasonable amount for support.

Suit for child support: A couple have separated, the children are with the mother, who sues the father for money to support them.

Suit for slander: One man claims that another has made untrue remarks that have injured his reputation and he sues for damages.

The list is endless, but these will give you an idea of the wide field that is open to the lawyer now.

Doubtless you are curious as to how much a lawyer earns. The answer was provided by the United States Department of Labor, which made a study of the earnings of more than 46,000,000 men whose occupations and salaries were given in the 1960 census.

The study, released in March, 1965, shows that only two

groups—doctors and business managers—have higher earnings than lawyers, who ranked third. The median earning
for 1960 was $10,557. Many salaries and fees have gone up
since 1960, and it would be a safe guess to fix the median
figure now at $11,000.

How much higher you can go will depend largely on you
and how hard you work. The future holds much promise, and
it is up to you to take advantage of the opportunities.

I wish you success—and satisfaction in your career.

# 35. The Future of the Law

Just what the future holds for the law and lawyers is anybody's guess, but if it is an educated guess, based on what we know now, it can foretell, in a broad sense, some of the things that lie ahead.

We know that the world today is moving in a certain direction: The population continues to increase; more machines are being created to provide more leisure for more people; people who have more leisure will have more time for good deeds or they will have more time to dream up ways to get into trouble; space is being invaded at an ever-accelerated pace.

These things we know now. We know that, if these thing continue to happen, but on a larger scale, another thing is certain: There will be more laws.

The more complicated our daily lives become, the more complex are the rules by which we live. More lawyers will be needed. They will be needed to draft laws, to help get them enacted, to interpret them after they have become statutes, to advise

clients who are affected by them, even to defend those accused of violating them.

Perhaps the twin dreams of World Habeas Corpus and international due process of law will come true. They certainly
won't be embraced by the whole world all at once, but one
nation after another will see the light until most, if not all, of
the countries of the world will recognize the dignity of the
individual and every person's right to due process of law.

The future undoubtedly holds many changes, some of
which are beyond our imagination. Space is a good example.
In the past ten years, we have witnessed feats in outer space
that would have been jeered at as impossible if someone had
suggested them even as recently as half a century ago.

What problems will the space age bring? Will the space-
ways become as cluttered as the airways are now? Will we
need a body of space laws to regulate traffic, to determine
which country shall use which space lanes at given times?
Who will be held responsible for damages to property and
injury to individuals in space? Who will have jurisdiction for
crimes committed in space?

Regardless of the rules, even some that are not conceivable
to us now, it is certain that lawyers will be the authorities
who will devise them. It seems quite likely that a lawyer
specializing in space law in the future also will need a degree
in physics or electronics.

But the greatest advance for lawyers of the future, the
greatest opportunities, lie in the field of public service. The
current programs of both state and federal governments are
aimed at more service to the public, or at least to certain seg-
ments of the public. These probably will grow rather than
diminish. You may find yourself, as an attorney for a big firm

or for a private individual, opposing some of them; or, as a lawyer for a government agency, fostering or defending them.

Even without a crystal ball, I feel safe in making some predictions:

The future with which you are concerned, that is, the years of your adult life, will not be dull.

And there will be a place for you, the lawyer, in this future, with almost unlimited opportunities.

# AFTERWORD

# 36. The Satisfactions of a Legal Career

The real rewards of a legal career are not in money. Undoubtedly, you will make a good living. You will earn enough to provide comfortably for yourself and your family. It is unlikely that you will become rich from the practice of law—although a knowledge of the law may help you to become wealthy through some other endeavor.

But your greatest compensations will come from within, a garland that will adorn your spirit, an accolade that will penetrate the innermost recesses of your heart, a great satisfaction that will encompass your career and enrich your life.

Even though you work alone, always at your side will be such constant companions as honesty, integrity and compassion.

You will glow with an inner warmth, whose flame never can be extinguished because:

You will give hope and help to the unfortunate.

You will defend with every ounce of your strength the cause of the weak.

You will devote all your skills and call upon hitherto unknown vitality to win freedom for the innocent.

You will fight for justice and against injustice wherever you may find it.

You will do your utmost to relieve distress and to melt despair.

You will bestow enlightenment upon the ignorant.

You will bring succor to the oppressed.

You will offer courage to the fearful.

Above all, you will deliver hope to the hopeless.

When at last you are compelled to quit, when your career is at its end, you will glance up at the shingle you hung out when you began your career. And you will be surprised:

The shingle is not dull and faded and lusterless, as you had supposed it would be. Instead, it is bright and shining, a brilliant lodestar beckoning other young men to a life of service to humanity.

Some, seeing that beacon, will remember why it is so bright:

You have helped others in many ways. You have been a strong and valuable influence in your community. You have helped to write laws for the betterment of humanity; you have helped to mold the better society of which you are a part.

You have influenced the course of history. When it paused, undecided, at the crossroads, you nudged it gently in the right direction.

Perhaps what you have accomplished will be recorded in

the history books, perhaps not. In your own mind and your own heart, you will know what you have done, and the memory will be reward enough. Surely, you will be proud and happy to be able to say, "I, the lawyer—"

# Index

237

# LUIS KUTNER

was born and brought up in the City of Chicago, of mixed ancestry—French, English, Spanish, German and Russian. Illness delayed his attendance at the public schools there until his ninth year, but he finished grammar and high school in seven years and entered the University of Chicago at the age of fifteen. All sorts of odd jobs helped to pay for his legal studies until he was admitted to the Illinois Bar. Even then, he lived on peanuts for weeks in order to be able to gain further knowledge in the office of a distinguished lawyer.

Early in his legal career, Luis Kutner began to dream of a World Habeas Corpus. Today, this tremendous undertaking is close to realization. This world-wide Rule of Law, for which he blueprinted a judicial structure and a procedure, has been acclaimed and endorsed throughout the world and the United States Congress as a universal Magna Carta. In 1952, he filed the world's first Petition for the United Nations Writ of Habeas Corpus in behalf of William N. Oatis, A-P correspondent, who was wrongfully imprisoned in Prague, Czechoslovakia. This led to the latter's release. He has also worked in behalf of Joseph Cardinal Mindszenty. He is the President of the Commission for International Due Process of Law, Chairman of the World Habeas Corpus Committee of the World Peace Through Law Center and travels intercontinentally in advocating the world collective responsibility for individual security.

Luis Kutner has been the recipient of many awards in recognition of his "Poor Man's Justice Program" and still manages to find time to help those who cannot afford legal advice or need rehabilitation. He is a former visiting Associate Professor of Law at Yale University and lectures in law schools throught the world. He is former Consul for Ecuador and Consul General for Guatemala.

Luis Kutner handles his wide range of hobbies just as enthusiastically and successfully as he does his legal profession. They are poetry, music, painting, sculpturing, history and athletics.

# *Luis* *Kutner*

s born and brought up in the City of Chicago, of mixed ancestry—French,
glish, Spanish, German and Russian. Illness delayed his attendance at the
olic schools there until his ninth year, but he finished grammar and high
ool in seven years and entered the University of Chicago at the age of
.een. All sorts of odd jobs helped to pay for his legal studies until he was
nitted to the Illinois Bar. Even then, he lived on peanuts for weeks in order
be able to gain further knowledge in the office of a distinguished lawyer.

Early in his legal career, Luis Kutner began to dream of a World Habeas
pus. Today, this tremendous undertaking is close to realization. This world-
le Rule of Law, for which he blueprinted a judicial structure and a proce-
e, has been acclaimed and endorsed throughout the world and by the United
tes Congress as a universal Magna Carta. In 1952, he filed the world's first
ition for the United Nations Writ of Habeas Corpus in behalf of William
Oatis, A-P correspondent, who was wrongfully imprisoned in Prague, Czech-
vakia. This led to the latter's release. He has also worked in behalf of
eph Cardinal Mindszenty. He is the President of the Commission for Inter-
ional Due Process of Law, Chairman of the World Habeas Corpus Commit-
of the World Peace Through Law Center and travels intercontinentally in
ocating the world collective responsibility for individual security.

Luis Kutner has been the recipient of many awards in recognition of his
or Man's Justice Program" and still manages to find time to help those
cannot afford legal advice or need rehabilitation. He is a former visiting
ociate Professor of Law at Yale University and lectures in law schools
ughout the world. He is former Consul for Ecuador and Consul General
Guatemala.

Luis Kutner handles his wide range of hobbies just as enthusiastically
successfully as he does his legal profession. They are poetry, music, paint-
sculpturing, history and athletics.